LEGS ON EVEREST

LEGS ON EVEREST

the full story of his most remarkable adventure yet

mark inglis

RANDOM HOUSE
NEW ZEALAND

To the past, the present and the future.
In memory of Dad (Jim); to Anne and my fantastic kids,
Lucy, Jeremy and Amanda — the journey continues.

A catalogue record for this book is available from
the National Library of New Zealand

A RANDOM HOUSE BOOK
published by
Random House New Zealand
18 Poland Road, Glenfield, Auckland, New Zealand

www.randomhouse.co.nz

First published 2006

ISBN-13: 978 1 86941 870 0
ISBN-10: 1 86941 870 0

Cover design: Katy Yiakmis
Design: IslandBridge
Printed in New Zealand by Publishing Press Ltd

Contents

Chapter 1

The dream

— and a taste of things to come

3am, 7 January 2002

Linda Glacier, Aoraki/Mount Cook, New Zealand

It's been 20 years since I last spent a night on this mountain. Back then, though, it was a very uncomfortable 13 and a half days huddled in an ice cave near the summit. Outside the longest storm in the area in recorded history raged, ensuring we went no further. Those nights and the resultant frostbite cost me both legs from below the knee.

No frostbite tonight, though it is just as cold and before me is something even scarier — the mountain that I failed on just three weeks ago. But I'm a tiger for punishment, so I'm back again with my good friends: Charlie Hobbs, my guide; Mark Whetu, our cameraman (and one of the toughest and best mountaineers around even with no toes, which he lost to frostbite in 1996); Mark Woodward (Woody), Whetu's 'safety' (also a very experienced climber, whose job is to look out for Whetu while he concentrates on getting the shots); and Wayne Alexander (better known as Cowboy), who's my leg guy. Three weeks ago I turned back with damaged stumps, and Woody guided Cowboy to the summit. Today it's my turn — Cowboy gets to play camp bitch for the day, though we just about need a chain to hold him back!

We've been climbing up through the night, weaving among crevasses that could swallow a house, pitch-black holes in the ever-steeper glacier. Thank Christ it's dark as we sidle up the nearly overhanging ledge they call the Linda Shelf, just the pinpoint of light below marking the place where Cowboy is keeping vigil. Above is the crux of the climb, the iced-up summit rocks — this is what I have waited 20 years for. The crux moves start with a sidle along an icy ledge with nothing but air for hundreds of metres below. Add to that some of the ice underfoot breaking away because of the crampon traffic that has already gone over it. The holds are a mix of 'dry tooling', a bit of ice where the tools bite in more securely, and a few handy jug- or crack-type hand-holds here and there. It's pretty exciting, and I surprise myself with some of the holds I manage, as if I'm rock climbing at home or on a wall. But this is the real thing, I think to myself. There's a tricky step up and around a bulge onto a steep ice slope, then a short vertical step, and the crux of the climb is dealt to. After that there are just over two rope-lengths of steep ice, a series of linked couloirs with short vertical steps in between.

By the time I'm halfway up that pitch I know the hill is in the bag, and I start to really enjoy myself. It's just a matter of time now — time and some serious sweat. The worst thing is that there are climbers above us who keep sending down ice and rocks. A nasty bit of ice hits me in the face and a rock crashes down onto my arm, but hey — I've done the crux!

Even then, I'm almost stopped by my right crampon. Those moves through the crux pitch have pushed it back on the foot, making front-pointing that much more difficult. The crampons I am trying out aren't working as I had hoped they would. I rely on my weight to get them to bite into the hard ice, but they aren't doing it. Hammering them in with a kicking motion would rapidly trash my stumps, so for the last pitch of the summit rocks I have to use the inside two points, which slows me down quite a lot. To add to the drama, every so often ice and rocks keep cascading down and I have to stop, hanging off my ice tools, shoulders hunched, as debris rains down, hitting my helmet with loud cracks and thuds. I think back to all those people who have asked if there is snow at the top of Aoraki/Mount Cook in summer — yes, there certainly is, although a lot of it has been knocked off and has landed on me today.

As you come over the top of the summit rocks you drop down a bit of hard ice to a col at the bottom of the ice cap. Looking up the ridge to the summit I can see a burning-hot trudge to come, interspersed with fluffy snow over hard ice. Though I can see the end, I know there's still a lot of hard work to be done.

The last 30 metres are a whirlwind of emotions. I'm smiling so much I think my face will crack. And for once I'm not even thinking about how I'm going to get down. If necessary I'll crawl or slide on my arse — it's all downhill. The final section disappears in a blink. I keep thinking of everything that has gone before, especially the attempt before Christmas, then my thoughts go to my wife Anne and our kids. But I know I can do it — nothing is going to stop me this time.

Everyone has huge grins on their faces — Charlie, Woody, Whetu and I — just as they do with every ascent of Aoraki/Mount Cook. It's always a buzz, even for those for whom climbing the mountain has become a job. For me there is also the relief, and a feeling of almost disbelief at how great it feels to be back. I am aware of the debt I owe to every person who has helped me get there, but also very conscious of a feeling of personal achievement, and a rising desire to go higher and harder.

Standing there is just like being on the podium to receive my silver medal at the 2000 Paralympics in Sydney — it's definitely the start of something, not the end. The top of a mountain is only halfway, after all.

Whenever you come out of the mountains, especially after you have pushed yourself to the limit, you have some of the wilderness in your heart, a drive and freedom that wasn't there before. You know you can achieve things that were once only a dream. And the more times you undertake the extreme journey, the greater your confidence that you will attain your dream, and the bigger your dreams.

As I passed Whetu to take the last couple of steps, all I could think of was, 'Hey, Stumpy and Gimpy on top of New Zealand — how about Stumpy and Gimpy on top of the world next?' If you want a bigger dream then go for the biggest — imagine standing on the summit of Everest!

23 August 2004

Since standing on the summit of Aoraki/Mount Cook two and a half years ago, every waking moment has been dominated by the dream I thought I had lost with my legs — a dream I found again on that summit: Everest. But life is about learning, and the last place to learn is in the death zone high on Everest. You need to learn on a mountain that you'll survive on if you stuff up. For me, that mountain is Cho Oyu. It is still a very serious undertaking, at 8201 metres the sixth highest mountain in the world. But it's the ideal training ground, where I will see whether I have the genes to acclimatise, the stamina to put up with the difficult and miserable conditions, and of course whether being a double amputee will be more or less of a disadvantage at altitude.

The year 2004 has been frenetic. Originally I had planned to climb Shishapangma, the Tibetan mountain that's the lowest of the 8000-metre peaks. After several people pulled out of the expedition at the last moment, leaving just Whetu and me, and maybe one other person, it

Climbing terms

ascender: a device that clamps onto a rope by means of spring-loaded jaws with teeth that slope back; these allow it to slide up the rope, but bite in and prevent it slipping down. They are used extensively in Himalayan climbing, much of which is done on fixed ropes. Using an ascender you don't need to be roped to your climbing partner; you are attached to the fixed rope instead.

belay: a system used to break a fall using the climbing rope. A fixed belay is when one climber is attached to the mountain while the other is climbing. A running belay is where both climbers, roped together, climb at the same time with the rope running through for protection (see below).

belay stance: an anchor position for the climber controlling the rope, ready to break the fall of the lead climber.

'on belay': this is called out once a climber has reached the belay stance and set up the protection to form the belay. When the other climber hears it, he or she knows to break down their belay system and start to climb.

col: a climber's term for a dip in a ridge, like a pass.

couloir: a snow- and ice-filled gully.

crux: the most difficult section or move of a climb.

dry tooling: using your ice tools as hand-holds on rock by hooking the points into cracks and notches.

seemed plain common sense to accept an offer from Russ Brice to join his 2004 Cho Oyu trip. Russ is the founder of Himalayan Experience (HIMEX), the leading expedition company on Everest, Cho Oyu and Shishapangma, which also arranges trekking throughout Tibet and Nepal. Joining him would give me a better chance of success and be far more cost-effective than climbing Shishapangma with such a small group.

Cost? Now that's the biggie. Do you know how many sponsorship

exposure: there are two meanings for this word in climbing. One means hypothermia, when your body can't create enough heat for the conditions, and it can kill you. The other meaning is the feeling when there are thousands of feet of space beneath your feet; you feel exposed, like being naked in a city mall!

freeze: like exposure, this has two meanings. Technique wise, it means not being able to move forwards or backwards, frequently just before you fall. Mostly it is used to describe the weather conditions. 'The Freeze' is essential and occurs when the temperature drops below 0°C, allowing the snow to freeze hard. This stops lots of small rock and ice falls, and allows you to climb on the hard surface rather than sinking in.

front-pointing: climbing steep ice and snow using both ice tools and the front (toe) points of the crampons (a frame of hardened steel spikes strapped to a climber's boot). Looks and feels like freezing-cold rock climbing.

pitch: a section of rock, snow or ice that is climbed between belay points, ideally about the length of the rope.

protection: any piece of equipment fixed to the rock or ice to anchor climbers or ropes to belay points. Commonly used protection includes nylon slings, snow stakes, pitons, nuts, cams and ice screws.

top out or summit: finish a climb, not necessarily at the top of a mountain.

traverse: moving across the mountain slopes, rather than straight up.

letters I wrote for Cho Oyu? Seventy-three. And do you know how many replies I got? Three! I was stunned at the rudeness of some of our biggest companies who didn't even give me the courtesy of a reply — even a 'No' is better than silence. Fortunately I was able to do several extra corporate-speaking jobs in the months before I left, filling the family coffers up somewhat, although it never seems enough at the moment.

It was during this time that our family faced one of its biggest tests, a test that happens every day to a family somewhere, and that is dealing with the death of a loved one. Dad's story is the story of a battle with cancer. And what a battle. It's an opponent that seems to have a never-ending arsenal to defeat you with. I know of many who have survived this battle, and as many who haven't won. The difference? Damn luck, I reckon. Sure, before you all bite my head off, everything that can be done needs to be done. From attitude to treatments, from the conventional to the mystical, every avenue needs to be explored. Hopefully one of those avenues, or several in combination, will lead to a pathway to newfound health. But for many like Dad, the avenues only have one end.

For four years Dad, with Mum at his side, battled down those avenues with characteristic strength and stoicism, but it seemed that every time they turned a corner, solved one problem, another appeared. The family had several calls to come to his bedside when the doctors decided there wasn't much time left, but they didn't know Dad. Somehow he would pull through, incrementally worse off each time but still fighting. But in June 2004 he was transferred to the Smith suite (a hospice unit) at the local nursing home in Geraldine, South Canterbury, where he and Mum lived. The 'death room', Dad called it. He had been adamant that he would never need it, regarding it as a failure in his fight against the enemy within. In many ways it was a relief to see him finally on a medication regime that eliminated his pain, but it was also a signpost that the end was near.

Mum and I were standing beside him as he took his last breath, a long rattling intake and a longer soft expelling of life — we knew it was coming, but that never makes it easier. Christ, he fought to the end, to the last second, to the last breath, never giving up. If that isn't one of the greatest gifts he could have left me then I don't know what is. If I can leave that same attitude as a gift for my family then I'll be a damned proud man.

Dad's death was even tougher for me than it needed to be as the day after he died I had to fly to Hamilton to do three days of corporate work. These were crucial to enable me to go to Cho Oyu and leave the family finances in some sort of health. Then it was back for the funeral at the end of the week. In the weeks that followed preparations for the trip took over my life.

The rushing around that goes on before a trip is always the worst time for everyone, and by mid-August Anne and the kids are in 'Bugger off, Mark' mode. This time it is perhaps even worse than usual, since I am not only trying to earn enough money to leave the family comfortable, but I am trying to get the concept of my sports food, PeakFuel, off the ground. As my departure draws near I'm shagged and hyped — a bad combination to be around, I can assure you.

At last 23 August arrives, and the panic of rushing around is soon over, for me at least. As usual it is tough to say goodbye to Anne and the family, especially with newspapers fighting for a quote (they got a good one from Anne — something like it's better that he is away climbing mountains than cluttering up home!). After tearing around Hanmer and Christchurch doing those last-minute things, then the last goodbyes, I am finally flying out of Christchurch for Auckland, the plan being to head on to Bangkok with Thai Airlines.

To cope with all the extra baggage climbing a Himalayan peak requires, and facing the thought of sleeping rough for the next six weeks, I had paid the extra to fly Thai Business Class. Luxury was what I was looking for, and luxury was what I missed out on — the plane was an old MD11 — jeez, I didn't realise planes that old were still flying. The service was excellent as always, but it was a bit like being on an old DC3 compared to the newer planes we have been spoilt with lately.

Auckland to Bangkok via Sydney, landing at 4.20am in the heat and humidity of Thailand. Hell, what a poxy time to arrive, and what a time to try to fit four big heavy kitbags and a pair of skis into a taxi, feeling hot, sweaty and shagged. Just to add to the excitement the taxi dropped me at the wrong hotel for a start, though it eventually dumped me and my circus at the Indra Regent Hotel in the centre of Bangkok.

24 August

The streets of Bangkok are a real revelation, far more aggressive than the stall-holders I had experienced in Cambodia the year before. The heat meant only short trips out onto the streets, including being suckered into a taxi tour of the driver's favourite (for that read 'backhand payment') places, and as always offering his sister at a super-special cut rate for a few hours (of what??). The main job for the day was catching up on some sleep and getting a haircut. Beware, though — a Thai number 4 cut is the equivalent of a Kiwi number 1! Oh well, it will be six weeks before I'm home again and the last thing I need is to be looking after hair.

25 August

Flight TG319 to Kathmandu at 10.30am is full of trekking and climbing types. Just three hours' flying on this last leg, with the excitement mounting. We land just after midday and I escape the crush of the airport to see Whetu, Russ and his sherpas waiting. For some reason, while I have never been here before, it immediately feels like home. We pile the kit on the roof of the wee van and head for Russ's 'base camp' in Kathmandu, the Hotel Tibet. It seems a funny name for a hotel in the capital of Nepal, until you get there and experience the hospitality and Tibetan culture there.

I am quite shocked at how hot and humid it is. It's damned tough as a double amputee surviving in this heat. I think there will need to be a significant intake of beer to control the body temperature. The stay in Kathmandu looks like being a tour of the world-famous (well, in climbing circles anyway) bars and restaurants — after a warm-up of pre-dinner drinks at the Red Onion bar (soon to become HQ) and dinner at K-Too in the Thamel district (the main tourist area). I feel lucky to have been 'blooded' in the markets of Cambodia — they make the bustle of Thamel seem like home, and pretty tame.

26 August

Back into the Thamel district to find the famous Shona's climbing shop and order the first down shorts ever to be made! Shona is a Sherpani (a female Sherpa) and her husband Andrew, though originally an Aussie, has lived in Nepal so long he's now Nepalese too — though he entertains

us as only an Aussie can. Red Onion of course for pre-dinner G&Ts —
this Kathmandu thing is very civilised, I must say — dinner at another
Kathmandu icon, Kilroys restaurant, with the evening finishing in the
traditional way — rickshaw races home.

27 August

My roommate Todd (Windle, that is, a mad Kiwi extreme skier) arrives,
sans luggage unfortunately for him. This is the start of a long, frustrating
and in the end disappointing crusade to find all his gear. Some airport
worker in Dubai or somewhere will now be the proud owner of a full
set of Himalayan climbing and skiing kit — not much use in the desert,
though. The only positive for Todd was that he was having his down suit
made at Shona's, hence it didn't disappear with the rest of his gear. Dinner
tonight at an awesome Chinese joint — the start of a lot of Chinese food,
I imagine, as we travel through Tibet.

28 August

A big day. Russ and Whetu are travelling overland with all the gear,
heading to Tingri, in Tibet, which is a two-day drive, then on to base
camp to set up. Travelling that way wouldn't give the rest of us mere
mortals time to acclimatise, so we'll fly to Lhasa, which is at 3600 metres
(Kathmandu is just 1200 metres), and gradually work our way up. We
head to the airport which, like any other airport in this part of the world,
is all about hurry up and wait. Lots of queueing, then a bit more waiting,
just for a change. But what an awesome flight! This time we're on an Air
China 757, and everyone's jostling for a window so they can gaze out at
Everest and Cho Oyu as we fly past.

After an hour-long flight we land at Lhasa International Airport,
though why they call it that I am not sure, as it is 93 km from Lhasa!
The jet parks out on the runway and we are jammed into buses before
being subjected to more waiting as we make it through immigration
and customs. At least here the temperature, and most importantly the
humidity, is just that much lower, unlike the altitude which is starting to
make my head spin. The flight gains you 2400 metres in one hour, with
the airport and Lhasa city at the same height as the summit of Aoraki/
Mount Cook.

As we exit the luggage hall — which is just that, a large hall with luggage spread all over the floor — we are met by our very well-dressed, very well-made-up and very aloof Chinese chaperone. She in turn introduces us to Nagwa, our Tibetan 'sirdar', who will accompany us on the Lhasa to base camp journey. It's part of Nagwa's job to shepherd us at all times, never letting us out of his sight. He hadn't been counting on a bunch of rebellious Kiwis though! The whole circus is theoretically controlled by the CTMA (the Chinese Tibetan Mountaineering Association), though the Chinese regard it as the CMA, and likewise if you're Tibetan it's the TMA — there's no love lost there.

Dinner in the Himalaya Hotel in Lhasa is like everything here — done as a group! It's also another fantastic Chinese meal. As I point out to the others, this isn't a climbing trip but a culinary journey across the roof of the world — way to go!

29, 30 August

Today we're cruising the streets and alleys of Lhasa visiting the many temples, as well as the Potala Palace, where we lose Todd, much to the consternation of our guides. Never mind, we tell them, he'll turn up some time before base camp, possibly — this causes even greater panic in the chaperone camp, a real highlight of the day! Still, it is a pretty neat feeling to be standing in the Dalai Lama's window, looking out on the square below. It's just a pity the view is dominated by a semi-circle of banks and department stores with an ugly 'freedom' statue in the middle. The really great statue in Lhasa is that of the Golden Yaks, which are huge beasts many metres tall. They're positioned in the middle of a roundabout, and are a beautiful sight.

31 August

Finally it's on the road to Shigatse, along the 'Friendly Highway' — well, actually the friendly goat track. The first 85 km or so is on a well-paved road, with lots of army trucks and freight trucks interspersed with wee garden tractors towing trailerloads of locals, a death-defying ride. Liberal use of the horn is essential, with passing manoeuvres that would make the cockiest boy racer pale with fright. The next 230 km, though, make up for the smooth tarseal — it's effectively the equivalent of a rough New

Zealand skifield road. We're lucky to make 50 kph at the best of times and that feels far too fast. Finally, though, there's some real height, with passes of 5300 metres and 4900 metres to negotiate. It's amazing to have cracked 5000 metres in height without ever leaving your seat.

Lunch is in a seriously dodgy dive, more like a shepherds' shack, where the choice is rice or potatoes with some boiled, foul-smelling yak. It takes some serious thought to decide whether or not to eat. I stupidly compromise and nibble — pretty dumb really, as either you put it in your mouth or you don't, and as soon as it's in then you may as well eat the lot. Survived it, but for the next seven hours in the jeep it nagged at me. I was waiting for that initial tummy rubble that would indicate the onset of 'thunder' activity like in Cambodia. I had vivid memories of just making it to my hotel room and spending the next 12 hours lying on the bathroom floor trying to work out which end was going to go first.

Yep, that's right, seven hours more of crawling across the Tibetan plateau, eventually striking a run of tarseal which meant Shigatse was imminent. The only paved roads and 21st-century facilities in Tibet are around the two cities, Lhasa and Shigatse, where the Han Chinese have settled. Elsewhere, even just metres outside of the city boundaries, you go back at least two centuries.

Hotel Mansoavaur in Shigatse is a walled compound, a haven of elegance and luxury. We have a fantastic meal that evening, Chinese yet again, but real Chinese like I have only experienced once before, in Cambodia of all places — the Chinese do get around. The next morning is spent juggling drivers as Todd, Jez (another climber) and I do a deal to get a different four-wheel-drive. Actually it was the driver we wanted to get rid of — he was too slow and dangerous. Fast and dangerous would have been fine thanks, and that was pretty much what we got with the new guy!

Then it's time to hit the food market. What a great market — much cleaner than the Cambodian ones, although this is more because of the weather than anything else, as it is less humid and much cooler here (though everything is relative; it would still make your average Kiwi shopper heave). Three whole yak legs and a couple of goat carcasses later and we are away again on another long drive. The pavement lasts only about 2 km this time, then it's back to the bone-rattling gravel road. We saw two graders on the road that day — well, sort of graders anyway — medium-sized rotary hoes (the standard mode of transport here) each towing a small grader blade, probably only a metre wide. Two of these for 300 km of rough road, plus work gangs with hoes and baskets — no wonder it's a goat track. I can't help thinking how Dad would react — after years as a grader driver, and being the perfectionist he was, it would have seemed a disgrace to him.

Just as it seems like the bucking and jolting will go on forever we hit another piece of pavement and roll into Old Tingri, the last town before base camp Cho Oyu. I don't know what the literal translation of Tingri is, but I think it should be 'shithole' — it will certainly always define that image for me. How do I describe it — a one-street town with the main Nepal/Tibet/China highway (the Friendship Highway) running through it, with the inevitable trucks belching clouds of dust, diesel and oil fumes, their horns blaring constantly to move the dogs, people, cows and horses off the road. The difference from other similar towns is that between the houses you can see Everest rising above the haze in the distance — a million-dollar view in a town you could probably buy for $100!

As you enter the town you drive through the rubbish dump, which is always full of rabid dogs, big mastiff-cross mongrels that dominate the night. The Everest View Hotel is a walled compound that used to be stables, and it's not far removed from that now. The gates are locked at night to keep both the dogs and the bandits out.

There are a few other expeditions here, one of which has a major problem. One of their members went out for an early morning walk and got bitten by a dog — in fact, he just escaped being mauled by the pack — and now he has to get anti-rabies shots. This would be very unpleasant at the best of times but here the nearest shots are in Kathmandu, 550 km of bad road away and across a closed border. Add to that the fact that there is an incubation time of seven days and he is in the poo. He's one seriously stressed guy, although very grateful that everyone is working hard to get the vaccination shots across the border. It's a tough position to be in at any time, let alone at the start of an expedition like this.

As I was standing in the morning light I was able to ring Anne while gazing at Everest — a very emotional call. Stupidly I also went for a morning wander. It was just after 7am, and while there were people up and about I still had to protect myself with rocks as the dogs took far too much interest in me. A strategic retreat to the hotel was called for. I may be a slow learner but I do learn!

The altitude of Tingri is about 4300 metres and I was feeling pretty comfortable with a resting heart rate of 75 beats per minute or so; not bad when at sea level I am about 60 beats per minute. It's time to stretch the legs after so long in the jeeps, and we do our first big walk here — 350 metres up to a sky burial site. Up there the heart rate is nearer 110 beats per minute — it's amazing what that little gain in altitude can do to the body. The rest of the party went on up to over 500 metres but I headed down as I am as slow as always.

3 September

Goodbye to Tingri thankfully and on to base camp today. Time to catch up with Russell and Whetu, who came through several days earlier to set up the camp with the sherpas. To my surprise it's a great road in. Apparently it is to become the new route to Nepal, but as always money has disappeared on the Nepalese side so several bridges aren't finished. Hence it is a road to nowhere at present, though one day it will be finished, they say.

I must admit the concept of driving to base camp will spoil me for expeditions forever. Sure, a ten-day walk in sounds glamorous, and potentially it is good training, but give me a jeep any day — I'm here to climb, not walk!

The Cho Oyu team

So who are we? Time to introduce the Cho Oyu team.

The guides
Russell Brice, aka Russ (expedition leader; most commonly known
    in Tibet and Nepal as 'Big Boss')
Mark Whetu ('Mark 1', a New Zealander)
Dean Staples ('Deano', another New Zealander)
Lydia Brady (New Zealander)
Jean Pavillard (Swiss/American; Monica Kalozdi's guide)
Thomas Torkelson ('Tom', American; Monica's guide and cameraman)

The climbers
David Bingham (Dave the Pom; 'I'm not a Pom, I'm from Cardiff')
Jeremy Benton ('Jez'; British, but we have decided he's an honorary
    Kiwi)
Akitomo Fujibayashi ('Mr Fujibayashi'; Japanese)
Chieko Shimada (Japanese)
Monica Kalozdi (American)
Charles Dasey ('Chuck', American)
Todd Windle (New Zealander; an extreme skier and climber)
and me, of course, aka 'Mark 2' or 'Zephyr'

As well as these, more climbers are due to arrive by the time we
get to advanced base camp (ABC in climbing jargon): Valerio Massimo,
known as 'the Italian prince', and Grania Willis, an Irish journo — it sure
sounds damned interesting!

The sherpas
Loppsang Temba Sherpa (sirdar)
Karsang Namgel Sherpa (high-altitude sherpa)
Lachhu Bahadur Basnet (ABC cook)
Kul Bahadur Magar (ABC cook)
Tibet Karsang (ABC cook boy and my sherpa)
Tibet Zambu (ABC cook boy)
Tibet Chuldim (BC cook boy/security)

Sherpas dedicated to Monica
Phurba Tashi Sherpa (high-altitude sherpa)
Chhiring Sherpa (high-altitude sherpa)

Structure of an expedition

In years gone by expeditions were almost invariably based around the concept of a team of climbers with one focus: for the fittest climber or pair of climbers to be put on the top — in much the same way as a cycle-racing team approaches the Tour de France, with everyone working for the most able.

In recent times things have changed, and many people now join commercial expeditions such as Russell Brice's Himalayan Experience trips to Cho Oyu and Everest. In these expeditions people from a wide range of backgrounds get together under the professional guidance of a team leader (such as Russ) and a number of guides, with the aim of getting everyone to the top. It's what I would call real teamwork. Being the stubborn bugger that I am, I make sure I am treated as just another member of the expedition — just another climber, another member of the team striving for the top.

A guide's job is not to drag anybody up the mountain, but to give direction and act as a sounding board, a source of information and advice. To get on a trip the climbers (or 'clients') have to apply and provide a climbing CV to ensure there are no 'surprises'. Because of this, and since the climbing is often on fixed ropes, the ratio of guides to climbers is generally one to four (or more than four); unlike alpine climbing, where the ratio is frequently one to one.

The real work is done by the sherpa staff and porters, who carry tents, sleeping bags and oxygen bottles to the camps high up on the mountain. Their role really hasn't changed in the history of Himalayan mountaineering, except that the sherpa staff are paid quite handsomely now, almost 30 times the average wage in Nepal or Tibet. High-altitude sherpas are also well-trained now, with climbing schools and certification in both Nepal and more recently Tibet, which in essence means their job has become much safer.

So in our expedition Russ is the Big Boss. We all — climbers, guides and porters — do as he says, or else!

Sherpa or sherpa?

'Sherpa' is actually the name of an ethnic group in Tibet and Nepal; the female is Sherpani. The Sherpas are well known for their mountaineering and trekking skills, and today the word 'sherpa' is widely used for a guide or mountaineer, particularly in the Himalayas.

Chapter 2

The learning experience

3 September

Cho Oyu base camp

It's fantastic to catch up with Whetu and Russ again, and we are all blown away by the amazing dinner our cook, Lachhu, has produced — huge sizzling platters of chicken, fresh salads, fries — the portent of good things to come.

In true Kiwi form we had celebrated Tom's birthday on our last night in Tingri with a bottle of Jack Daniels, hence some people were somewhat subdued that first night at base camp. I had a terrible night, spending most of it scared witless as I gasped for breath. This was my first experience of Cheyne Stokes breathing, the interrupted breathing pattern of altitude. I must have been awesomely well-hydrated, though, as I filled the pee bottle to the rim and almost — I stress almost — to overflowing.

4 September

Tired and worried in the morning but apparently that's normal. The first yak train departs for advanced base camp. What a great sight, watching Russ and Loppsang, his sirdar, negotiate the load sizes and weights, then the yaks being loaded, then their procession out of camp up the valley towards the glacial moraine. Another acclimatisation climb today, this time up to 5100 metres. Things are starting to feel pretty good really.

The afternoon is spent sorting kit with Whetu and working on the climbing legs — making sure things like the crampons fit properly, cutting more and more off the soles to make them lighter, and drilling more holes in them to get them lighter again. Also tried to use my laptop but unfortunately it has died, no way would it boot up. It tried manfully but 4650 metres seems to be its limit — it might be the cold, the dust or just the altitude.

What is Cheyne Stokes breathing?

When you breathe you convert oxygen to carbon dioxide, and it is the build-up of carbon dioxide in the blood that is the key signal to the brain that it is time to breathe. If the carbon dioxide level is low, the drive to breathe is blunted (the lack of oxygen is a much weaker signal, and acts as the ultimate safety valve). As long as you are awake it isn't much trouble to breathe consciously, but at night an odd breathing pattern can develop due to a back-and-forth balancing act between these two respiratory triggers. Periodic breathing consists of cycles of normal breathing which gradually slows, then breath-holding, and a brief recovery period of accelerated breathing — panic!

This is not a form of altitude sickness, but just the body's way of compensating for low levels of oxygen, something that happens rarely to most people. The breath-holding phase may last up to 10–15 seconds, and while it may improve slightly with acclimatisation, it does not usually resolve itself until descent.

This periodic breathing situation can cause a lot of anxiety:

- In the person who wakes up during the breath-holding phase and knows he or she has stopped breathing;

- In the person who wakes up in the post-breath-holding hyperventilation (recovery) phase and thinks he or she is short of breath and has High Altitude Pulmonary Edema (HAPE — more on this later);

- In the person who wakes up and realises his or her neighbour has stopped breathing.

In the first two cases waiting a few moments will establish a normal breathing pattern, though they can be a frightening few seconds. In the third case, the sleeping neighbour will eventually take a breath, though periodic breathing cycles will likely continue until he or she is awake.

5 September

What a great night. Had an excellent sleep — it must have been the few beers that helped. Bed tea is brought at 7am whether you like it or not! In fact, you need to get back into bed for it otherwise Lachhu tells you off.

Everyone is up early, itching to get going, but we have several more days here yet. With every day here you feel a bit stronger and fresher. Up to 5050 metres today to practise fixed-rope climbing with an ascender, making sure everyone knows how to climb safely, clipping on and off the fixed lines. I must admit to feeling a wee bit nervous and unsteady up on the rock ledges where we are doing it, and hope it's just the altitude making the brain a bit tender.

6 September

Yep, another day at base camp. As always, 7am Sherpa milk tea (hot sweet milky tea). It is still very easy to run out of breath; God knows what it is going to be like further up. I spend some time setting up the skis and having a few hours on the climbing legs, then it's time for another walk up the hill. Todd, Chuck, Jez, Dave and I head up the slopes above camp — great walking on grassy ledges among bluffs and shale slopes. I stopped at 5250 metres and read a book for a few hours while the others went higher. Chieko went to 5650 by herself! She's one tough lady.

ABC barrel time. This means it's time to pack up everything you will need for three to four weeks on the hill, but it has to be less than 30 kg, which is half a yak load. What to take? It's just like leaving home

---

Barrel time

An expedition barrel really is a barrel, but rather than a wooden one filled with wine — the sort of barrel I am most used to — these are 100 to 130 litre blue plastic barrels with lids that seal with a band and padlock. The general rule for kit is that if it can fit in the barrel then you can take it, with a maximum weight of 25–30 kg, depending on the condition of the yaks at the time.

---

in Hanmer Springs — it's time to pack and repack, then repack again just to be sure.

As the cellphone won't work from here it's time to try the satellite phone, but to no avail. Eventually I do get through to Anne but the line is terrible. It's bloody difficult to talk too, as there is a long lag phase — we both find it very tough, very frustrating.

7 September

ABC day — about time. A second yak train will also come up, and though they head out in the early morning we pass them during the first 13 km as we're bouncing around in the back of a dump truck! The truck gets us right up beside a lateral moraine of a glacier that traverses our path — thankfully, as it would have been a bugger of a walk for me otherwise. I was one grateful double amputee, I can assure you.

From there it's on foot, and most people take off like sprinters, just a few of us cruising at the back. It is very difficult walking — typical of moraine, with big boulders that are very unstable — though occasionally there is a defined path thanks to the yaks. About four and a half hours later I wobble into ABC feeling pretty unstable. I certainly didn't eat or drink enough — stupid really, as I should know better. Lachhu and Karsang had a very welcome cup of Sherpa tea for Whetu and I about 30 minutes before ABC. This was a life-saver, not just for the tea, but as an excuse for a stop. The yaks passed us about 20 minutes before we got in — damn, beaten by the yaks! Most of the team did a quick three- to four-hour walk, which is almost half the time taken by other teams. This is a real testament to the programme of acclimatisation Russ has had us on.

ABC, time to chill out again. It's actually much easier to chill out here as it is starting to get really cold, with the odd snow flurry overnight to chill the place down as well. I'll be here for at least a week, the plan being to do acclimatisation walks most days, eat well and sleep well — that's the plan, anyway.

9 September

Time is slipping by. It's time for the first big walk, up to lake camp on the way to camp 1 (C1 in climbers' jargon). Well, not quite all the way for me. I'll see lake camp soon enough as I will be sleeping there for a night or two. Russ, Whetu, the sherpas and the yak boys all head on higher up the hill with loads to C1 — jeez, Russ is tough.

It's the usual bloody nightmare of a trip for me. While the gain in elevation to where I stopped is modest it didn't stop me from puffing hard, but the trip down was the killer. The difficult moraine and going downhill is the worst combination for me, and the less I need to do it the better. Even getting around ABC can be difficult. When the rocky ground is lightly covered with fresh snow overnight it makes for slippery footing, especially with all the unstable rocks disguised.

I must admit, though, that there is nothing like fresh snow to clear my mind and perk up my thoughts. The thing I am discovering is that you really need either high altitude or drugs to dream amazing dreams (though I wouldn't know much about the drugs, honest). I'm having crazy dreams up here, though for every great, exciting dream there is also the worst nightmare you will ever have.

11 September

Grania and Valerio (the Italian prince) were due in today. Knowing how grateful I was for the milk tea and bikkies Lachhu brought down when I was on the way up, I did the sherpa thing and went to the end of the lateral moraine to meet them. The bikkies and chocolate went down a treat but they weren't so keen on the tea. Oh well, they will soon learn to like it!

13 September

Todd and Jez do a big walk today right over the glacier towards Nang Pa La (the pass that links Nepal to Tibet, a traditional yak caravan route) then on to the end of the lateral moraine. Watching them disappear was fascinating as it really gave some scale to the mountains and glaciers here. Again I made like a sherpa and headed down the moraine track to meet them, but this time with black coffee, bikkies and some other treats. The walk down was pretty good for me actually, not quite dancing down the track, but not far away. The track is much better now thanks to the heaps of yaks that have brought other expeditions' kit up to ABC. On the way back up I almost kept up with them, but only because Todd wasn't trying. Jez was, though — he definitely needs to be first!

Time to experience the legendary guides' party in the 'homestead' (the guides' tent) — I think they call it the daily planning meeting. Whisky with honey is the order of the day, though it's a beer for me after that as after one whisky I was just about legless — wrong, I *was* legless. To add insult to injury, as I stumble on the snow-covered rocks back from the store tent the can of Pabst beer in the pocket of my down jacket explodes! Now I will smell of Pabst piss for the rest of the trip — bugger.

Chapter 3

Cho Oyu

— the roof of the world

14 September

It's time to leave the comfort of ABC and do what I came to do — climb. Time to head up towards camp 1. I'm heading out a day earlier than the others as I will stay at lake camp for the night with Karsang, my sherpa. Then in the morning, hopefully with fresh legs, I'll tackle the formidable 300 metre high scree slope that leads up to camp 1.

My heart rate is at 80 beats per minute in the morning. ABC is at 5660 metres and lake camp is only at 6010 metres, so it's just a wander really. A very cold morning greets us, and as always at the start of these big challenges I am feeling very nervous. My stumps are cold and quite tender. Whetu is planning on coming up part-way and doing some filming, and Tom has the whole team together to do an intro piece for Monica's 'home movie' (her home movies have bigger budgets than most docos I've ever done). It's certainly shaping up to be a camera day.

Contact with home has been patchy and difficult, and it's even more so this morning. I'm using Russ's laptop to try to send a return email to Anne, covering a range of concerns, including that big bogie, money — well, no money in this case actually — when the laptop battery dies. Bugger, you just don't need that sort of complication on a day like today. I got part of a reply off but it has left me feeling very stressed and a bit tearful — what a wimp. Nothing like making a hard day harder. The stress has certainly shown up in my pulse rate going way up and the psoriasis that I suffer from getting much worse.

There's time to take the walk up the moraine slowly, and there is no sense in rushing. The lake camp tent is right at the bottom of the dreaded scree slope, up on a rise big enough that the boulders that tumble down from hundreds of metres above don't quite reach us, though they sure give it a great try. The afternoon is spent watching members of other groups virtually crawl up the scree slope, and feeling very glad that I don't need to do it right then and there.

Todd and Jez had kindly offered to cart some kit up the next day, but I discover that in the panic of trying to sort gear in the morning and do the email thing I have given them the wrong bag. Hence I have no headlamp, and no ibuprofen for the splitting headache. Since it is dark at 7pm it's going to be a long night. Karsang is ripping up some dried mutton to make a sheep soup for his tea, but I'll stick to tomato soup and a can of tuna, I think. There's a radio check-in at 6pm — Karsang can do that as it is too bloody cold out there and I'm travelling light.

15 September

Luckily it is light just after 5am, and by 6.30 I'm ready to go. Karsang wants to wait for the others, but no way. I don't mind getting into camp last but buggered if I will start out last. Boil the billy, breakfast of tomato soup with bits of canned ham floating in it — the breakfast of champions! I pack up my kit, leaving Karsang with a bag of video gear and other bits and pieces. I must admit that he doesn't look too happy about that, but never mind, that's what he's being paid for.

Then it's up the dreaded scree slope. It's a bit of an anticlimax really, and no different from hundreds of similar slopes in New Zealand. It has a decent track up (for a scree slope, anyway) and my La Sportiva Mega super-light climbing boots work a treat. Before long sherpas and yak boys start heading past me, though they are all working just as hard as I am, and breathing just as hard. The big difference is that they are each carrying 30 kg and I only have about 8 kg. Once again you need to remember — their job, my hobby!

As I crest the top of the scree slope, camp 1 is laid out below. Yeehah! Then there's a tricky sidle down a steep icy slope to the main camp, where there are already at least 20 tents. Karsang has now caught up with me, and as I hunt for Russ's distinctive yellow tents he points up over the next knoll. I trudge on up, thinking that I should have known better — Russ always has the highest camp. Finally, snuggled into a small saddle is our camp, with its ten HIMEX tents all set up. Yay, I get first choice for a change, I think. But no, I'd forgotten that everyone else has been here a few days ago and booked their tents. Fortunately Chuck (my tent-mate for the rest of the time on the mountain — poor Chuck!) had picked a pretty good one in the centre of the cluster.

I'm now at 6350 metres. What an awesome place! I'm sorry if 'awesome', 'fantastic', 'amazing' seem to litter the text, but it really is that sort of place. The rest of the team turn up at about midday and settle in. Russ does things differently from other people, smartly. At each camp (1, 2, 3) there is one tent for every two team members. In each tent there are two sleeping bags and accompanying sleeping mats, a Primus, gas canisters for it, a billy and matches — the elements of survival at any altitude; well, on any mountain really. All you need to carry for yourself is your climbing kit, oxygen kit and food. Yep, you are responsible for feeding yourself. It's actually really smart, as up here no one knows what they want to eat, everyone is different, and this way you can take what you want. If you don't like it you only have yourself to blame!

16 September

I wake from one of the best night's sleep I have had since I left home. Sharing with Chuck is a real delight, though his blue lips look worrying. (They're the result of lack of oxygen; though I don't know it, mine are probably as bad or worse.) I try not to focus on them when chatting but it's tough — a bit like not looking at an awesome cleavage really. The best thing about Chuck is that he *snores*. Yes! Now I don't need to feel guilty about my chainsawing at night. The big surprise to me, though, is that I am hardly snoring at all — me who's had only half of one nostril working all my life, and in a place where you need every hole possible to suck in oxygen. Whatever works, I guess. The secret may be one ibuprofen before bed, but possibly more important is the extensive picking and blowing of the nose — yep, altitude is gross, sorry about that.

The only problem here is that I am not peeing enough, so I need to be drinking heaps more fluid. I also need the others to bugger off first, as I am really looking forward to my time alone up here.

Camp 1 is on an arête that leads up the northern face of Cho Oyu.

It is mostly ice, with rocky outcrops, and scalloped into a series of steep steps, linked by little 'flat' sections. Today everyone is heading up towards the ice cliff. Breakfast is sharing Alpine Granola with Chuck, hot Nestlé 'coffee and milk', then it's time to go. As always it's very cold until the sun hits at about 8am. It really is amazing watching lots of other climbers in full down suits — I am overheating in just my fleece top. The guides try to explain that they will overheat in down, but people don't seem to listen.

Equally incredible is that several people's crampons don't fit! They have new Millet Onesport boots — specialist high-altitude boots — but they haven't tried their crampons on them. The guides are starting to lose their cool with them, so it is definitely time to get the hell out of here. I don't have any patience with these people any more. The yelling starts as I leave camp and head up, with Jez and Todd following.

To say the air is a bit thin would be a significant understatement, but I am feeling pretty damn good. It's nice cramponing on firm snow and I'm really in my element. I start to pass a few climbers from other expeditions and play yo-yo with a group of sherpas, carrying big loads as always — it's a tough job! Within 20 minutes I am down to just two layers: a light merino base, with a light 'windstopper' top.

What looked to be an undulating ridge from ABC turns out to be 300 metres of steep steps. One set has two pitches of fixed rope up it for safety, while the others are just short 40-degree steps joined by flattish sections of ridge. It's one and a half hours to the ice cliff, and I'm going well. Todd and Jez pass me just before the last slope leading up to the cliff, and I realise I must be going strong to have kept in front of them for so long. Russ, Whetu and Deano are topping out on the ice cliff as we arrive. There are already several fixed ropes on the cliff, which is about a 30 metre vertical section that has to be climbed up and rapped down (aka rappelling or abseiling), and the idea is that they will fix a new route off to the left of the main cliff. That way there won't be any traffic jams when some people are wanting to go up while others want to come down — smart, huh?

As always Todd and Jez are in a hurry and go straight up the cliff — anything to be first! The only trouble is that Russ needs us to help with making the route up the rising traverse he is in the process of fixing.

Needless to say some choice phrases are directed at them. The result is that muggins here is the first climber up the new route. Generally this would not be a problem, but the main part of the traverse is waist-deep sugary powder over blue ice. I drop at least 3 metres down the almost vertical slope before the crampons can bite, then I have to climb up the steep steel-hard blue ice to get back on route. It's one of the toughest things I have ever done and I'm gasping and panting, but eventually I get back on line. Dave ('I'm not a Pom, I'm from Cardiff') is coming up behind me so I warn him, but it goes in one ear and out the other. An added complication is that he can't front-point for shit (sorry, that's a technical climbing term). I'm gasping for air and yelling instructions in terminology that even he is starting to grasp (it really does involve some seriously colourful language) but to no avail. For the sake of everyone else and the formation of the route Lydia has to climb up and help him, which is a bit of a bloody worry this low down on the hill. All this time I have a 'pole cam' on. This is one of Whetu's bright ideas — a mini digital video camera mounted on a pole that is attached to my pack. Well, my language should make for a few 'beeps' if they try to use it in a doco.

Just as I near the last anchor changeover (where the fixed rope is attached to an ice screw) I drop through the powder again, only this time I am wallowing chest deep. I'm almost vomiting with the effort, and I look up to find myself staring straight down the lens of Whetu's camera. How come he always manages to be in the wrong place at the wrong time (well, a cameraman calls it the right place, the right time)?

Hell, this is only the practice day!

I finally join the terrible duo, Todd and Jez, who are soaking up the sun on the top of the ice cliff wondering where everyone else is. They are near the abseil point and I congratulate them on their avoidance skills.

By the time the rest of the team have arrived the new route looks like a highway. We rap down and start what is always the worst part of any day for me — the trip down. Whetu stays close as always, and Lydia is 'tail-end Charlie', so we have a very social, chatty time as I hobble down.

Three steep steps before camp 1 I hear the dreaded 'ping', one of the two 'ankle joint' bolts shears and one of my feet goes seriously floppy. Whetu calls Russ to get one of the boys to rummage through my leg bag and get the spare bolts, spanner and an Allen key. It would have been

The Cho Oyu team assemble outside 'base camp' Kathmandu, the Red Onion bar, August 2004.

Whetu, Shona and Andrew in the most cramped climbing store in the world, 'Shona's'.
Shona is a magician, whipping up my down shorts overnight.

Sorting the expedition barrels at base camp, Cho Oyu.

Yaks each carrying 60 kg up the unstable glacial moraine to Cho Oyu ABC (advanced base camp).

The Cho Oyu puja ceremony at ABC, with Cho Oyu in the background;
the route goes straight up the face seen here.

Karsang climbing up the dreaded scree
slope towards camp 1.

Climbers slowly ascend towards the ice-cliff
on Cho Oyu between camps 1 and 2.

Standing on the roof of the world, Cho Oyu, 27 September 2004 — an awesome birthday present.

Teelay walks for the first time in 20 years.

Everest from the summit of Cho Oyu — only 649 metres higher, just one more day's climbing!

good to have hooked up a short rope in case the last bolt broke and I went for a tumble, but no rope! What sort of guides are these? Guides my arse! Lydia climbs just below me on the fall line so if I do go for a skate at least she will have a go at grabbing me, and Whetu is right behind, ready to grab my pack.

Twenty minutes later Russ arrives with the leg kit. Ten minutes of work and the broken leg is fixed. Try doing that with bones, you guys!

Some thought now needs to go into ensuring the same thing doesn't happen again higher up on the hill. The problem is that the alloy pylons (a bit like your shins) have a bevelled leading edge so they can be put into skiing mode, and this means there are some big shear forces on the bolts. I have a plan, though. Just behind the pylon there are holes drilled to lighten the legs. If I can get one of these to accept a bolt, therefore preventing the movement and eliminating the shear forces on the bolt — well, it will be a done deal.

Camp 1 is full that evening, and as I've said I just can't wait for the others to head away so I can focus on the job in hand and also have the whole tent to myself. Yes, selfish I know — 'No-friends Mark', as my family would say.

17 September

I wake up to a great day again, the third day in camp 1. A rest day for me, though the rest of the team pack up and head down the hill to the comfort of ABC for the next week at least. Most people acclimatise most comfortably by staying at ABC, with trips up to camp 1, especially if it is their first high-altitude expedition. Me, I can put up with the discomfort if it means no extra descending. As a double amputee most damage is done to the stumps when I'm going down — add the fact that it also takes more energy to descend, then the less of it I have to do the better.

It's time to sort out the tent, do an inventory of the food, and compile a list of things for Lachhu to send up with the sherpas as they come past carrying loads for higher up the hill. I've had to leave behind at ABC my barrel with extra books and the comforts of home, but every three days Karsang comes up to resupply me with food and bring up treats.

The biggest problem up here is that there is no contact with Anne and the outside world. I have a radio so I can talk to ABC (with 7am and 6pm radio schedules each day) but no phone yet, though Russ promises to send one up. The best I can do for the moment is to write an email note for Russ to send home for me.

One of my self-imposed duties is to make like a café for our team, as there is a constant stream of our sherpas coming by, going both up and down. The idea is to always have boiled water ready for rehydrating, the Primus ready for tea-making, and Whetu has lent me his espresso kit, so I'm a high-altitude barista as well. Jean, Tom and Monica come by today; they spent the night at camp 2 and appreciated a fresh coffee on the way home.

By midday the snow has started, with light cloud swirling around. Lunch at Café Camp 1 consists of hot pizza and an espresso — tasted fantastic, thanks Whetu. (The technique for the pizza is to use the billy lid to heat it up while it is still wrapped in tinfoil, but I burnt its arse so will need to work on a better system.) What a difference it made once everyone was gone. I settled into the continual task of preparing water so that I could keep the drink bottle and thermos flask filled. The evening radio schedule was more about passing on messages from the sherpas to Russ than anything else. Food consisted of three mini pizzas (which I had scoffed by evening), four biscuits and six bits of chocolate. It feels more and more like Middle Peak Hotel (the ice cave on Aoraki/Mount Cook where I spent 13 and a half days in 1982) by the hour!

18 September

7am and radio schedule time. It feels even more like Middle Peak because the bloody radio will only receive and not send. I'll need to be out on the ridge for each radio schedule to have any hope of communicating. I put in an order for some Dettol soap to ensure no bugs sneak up on me.

Lots of people are heading up, but the weather is closing in, with high winds further up the mountain causing huge plumes of spindrift to stream off the ridges. Valley cloud swallows the camp by mid-morning. I'm on water duty again for the sherpas coming by, and espresso duties for myself — no food, so I sure hope Karsang turns up some time as promised. I must admit I had a great night. With the whole tent to myself I have Chuck's sleeping mat (and a few from the other tents as well — just don't tell Russ) and his sleeping bag under me, and my sleeping bag is like a duvet on top. The inside of the tent really does look like a rat's nest but it sure is comfy, and that's what matters here. I think I desperately need a shave as I can feel some serious patchy bum-fluff on the face — I must look terrible.

At 11.45am Karsang, my saviour, arrives with food and the satellite phone — two tins of tuna, one tin of ham, potato cakes, one packet of biscuits (I asked for four), four cakes of chocolate (I asked for one, so I can feel a mochaccino coming on), a litre of Sherpa stew and, best of all, four cans of Lhasa beer! Tried the satellite phone and guess what, the network was busy! They forgot to send books up so I sent Karsang home with another shopping list comprised of boiled eggs, books and the soap, also forgotten.

I finally got the phone to work and contacted Anne. I have arranged for her to call me between 1 and 3pm each day my time, early evening her time. Even the radio worked tonight for a change — about time.

19 September

Day 5 in camp 1 and I had a pretty good night's sleep. I woke a couple of times, more out of boredom than anything, then woke with a start at 7.20am. It's very cold outside. There are two teams going for the summit and the radio call is due at 8am, so I throw the legs on and climb up onto the ridge, freezing my arse off. 8am, no call. By 8.11 I call them and get Lachhu. No one is up yet at ABC; it seems that during the night I have bumped my watch onto time 2, an hour out! At the real 8am I chat again to Deano, ask for books, pretty please; it's cruel punishment having to reread the same book time and time again. It's cold and misty in the valley apparently, but lovely and clear up here.

10.30am, climbing legs on and up the hill. I climb to a rocky outcrop two steps above my camp, about 200 metres up I guess. Slow and steady is the name of the game here. The radio works much better up here as it is in line of sight to ABC, so I have a great chat with Whetu. It is such a nice day, cool but clear, so off come the top clothes for a spot of sunbathing while I read the book again. It's a bit of a dag really — here I am sunbathing in shorts and no top, and all the while other expedition teams are climbing by in their down suits — what is wrong with these people?

After an hour or so it's time to head down back to my chores, mainly topping up the water supply (I've just finished the first gas canister, which is pretty good going really). Two sherpas yell out on the way past — they have brought up my four hard-boiled eggs from ABC. I am pathetically grateful. I'm becoming addicted to them actually. Now all I have to do is take a plastic bag and put some salt and pepper in it, throw in an egg, then later in the day at a rest break take the egg out, peel it (it's OK, you can throw the shell away, it will biodegrade), drop the egg back in the bag and give it a shake. Awesome! It really is a sad state of affairs when that is all that excites you. I managed a couple of eggs and a cup of tea for lunch, a few slices of canned ham (fried in the billy lid) and a squashed crumpet for afternoon tea.

Anne rang at 1.15pm; nice to hear her voice. I have had to sort through the Sherpa stew, picking out the potatoes and meat. The rest — mostly consisting of chilli — went to the crows. They are big buggers; they look like the ravens at the Tower of London. I'm sure they could do you some serious harm if they were hungry enough. Later I chatted to Deano again on the scheduled radio call; he must have drawn the short straw again. He promised to send up a new book — I'll be glad of that, as I'm on the fourth reread of John Grisham's *The Rainmaker*.

It looks as if the team will come up on the 21st or 22nd to head for the summit. That's good, it's about time to get the bloody show on the road. Back up to the start of the fixed ropes — I really thought I would run up by now but no way, it's still bloody tough. The air is just so, so thin. It's interesting watching the sherpas though. Everyone seems to think they have some magic gene that lets them perform at altitude, whereas my conclusion after observing them over the last few days is that they are just bloody tough. They are hurting as much as anyone, but they get on with it. Amazingly, some stop by the tent and pull out a packet of fags and light up! Christ, I can hardly breathe and here they are smoking. At 7 in the evening my heart rate is 76 — not bad at all for 6350 metres. I scoff my last Lhasa beer and reread the bloody book again — the nights are very long.

20 September

The sixth day in camp 1. This morning I woke to new snow and high cirrus clouds with hogsbacks forming — a big storm on the way, I think. It's a strange morning — it's snowing but the sun is shining at the same time.

I had a chat to Russ on the radio from 100 metres up the hill. There are no climbers coming up for a few days but he is sending Karsang up today. I put my order in for soap, a book and some bread type of food. An old dude heads up the hill past the tent; he must be 70 at least and he looks like death. Every step was followed by a pause for five seconds or so, and I could hear his rasping breath. He had one sherpa in front, tied to him, and one behind, fully loaded and pushing! It's 10am already, hot, and he is heading to camp 2 apparently. Not likely! I headed up the hill as usual, today trying one of the sherpas' ice axes. It's a bit heavy but with its long straight shaft it's a much better tool than my stupid technical axe. I'll need to see if I can borrow one as it feels much safer than just poles up on the steep stuff.

Karsang arrives with a 'gift box' that includes my bathroom kit (I can now shave and wash — almost don't stink), bread rolls, butter and jam, and a new book, *Cold Mountain*. Two Norwegians have moved into the neighbourhood, setting up their tents just behind mine. They tell me there are two days of bad weather coming — bugger.

It's now 17.17, 43 minutes to radio time, not that I'm counting of course. No phone call from Anne or Norm, my friend and business partner, who had said he was going to ring today. I must admit I am feeling pretty proud of my solo marathon up here; it makes me feel much better about not carrying much up the hill. The food has been interesting — some great, some crap.

21 September

My seventh day at camp 1. My heart rate this morning is 80 beats per minute. There was a really big storm last night, with awesomely high winds buffeting the tent all night — just what I enjoy, hence I must admit I slept well. The bloody radio is piss poor again this morning, and I also need to hear from Anne with numbers for me to ring if I ever make it to the top.

Had the dreaded dump this morning. Christ, I hate shitting in the mountains, trying to squat and not get anything on your clothes, just finding a place to do it away from camp, away from the climbing route. Fingers freezing, butt freezing, then clean yourself up — yuk, I hate it. The less I eat the less I shit — that's a good thing at this stage of the game.

It's washing day at 6350 metres. I will be interested to see if my undies and other clothes dry up here. Although it is sunny and there's a breeze, the temperature is down at 5°C or so. There are some huge hogsbacks over the summit of Cho Oyu and the clouds are scudding by the tent here, so I think we're in for some real 'weather'.

The Norwegians are full of questions. They're nice guys but are getting to be a bit of a pain. John Cook, the old dude, came past again, again being towed up the hill. He just wants to make 7000 metres while he is 70 — good on him if he can, though I wouldn't put dollars on it. I went up to the fixed ropes again; no faster, which is frustrating, but I am definitely recovering more quickly.

The bloody batteries in the radio are rooted, won't hold a charge, and of course everyone is giving 'useful' advice. What do they think I am, dumb or something? I was somewhat short with the team on the radio, but who cares. I've been here too long now. I think my physical performance has plateaued but my mental performance is definitely going downhill.

Norm rang from New Zealand, and unfortunately I was very short with him. All I could think at the time was 'Do you guys not know how hard it is to live up here?' Every little thing is becoming a problem.

22 September

My eighth day here. Last night was a wild one, with huge winds buffeting the tent again. Although I do love a great storm I did get the legs ready for a quick trip out, as for a while there it looked like the tent would go. There was no snow with the storm, but I wake to a world that is frozen solid. The head is feeling really heavy this morning but the heart rate is down to 63 beats per minute, which means I'm walking around OK but mentally going downhill I think. Did the dump thing again this morning — actually one of the more successful ones, if I may say so — though no dump would be even better. The food is down to a few digestive bikkies and some Japanese dehydrated stuff that I am never going to eat, there's no radio, no phone (network down), so not much of a morning really.

By early afternoon two sherpas, Monica, Tom and Jean have arrived with pizza, pasta and Coke — just what the doctor ordered. Apparently Chuck and Dave are coming up too, and the rest of the team tomorrow, with all of us looking to summit on the 26th. About bloody time.

Chuck arrives at 2.20 just as it is starting to snow heavily, then Dave appears out of the storm looking his usual myopic self. Annoyingly, he then proceeds to do a video diary, a steady moaning about everything in his Welsh accent. Chuck makes use of one of the other tents tonight but comes over for dinner. It is time to plan and order up food for camp 2 and camp 3. I will need some carbohydrate to recharge the muscles, a bit of protein to rebuild the muscles, and lots of fluids. The toughest thing about camp 3 will be just stomaching it.

The team that has moved in next door spend all night bed-hopping by the sound of it. A multiple-partner thing going on at 6350 metres — very distracting.

23 September

Day 9 in camp 1. I got up early to go do the dump thing as we have a 'toilet' now, a low snow-block wall with a bag in a hole to crap into. I managed to use it without messing myself or falling in, so a very successful trip really. Tea and chocolate for breakfast. I sure hope Russ and the rest of the team get up here with some real food soon. The head is feeling really heavy and the nostrils are blocked, which means even more gasping. There isn't enough loo paper to blow the nose (it's a very precious commodity up here; I only have two rolls left) so there is a lot of one-nostril blowing — the difference is a clear head, and a clear head means clearer thinking.

A bit of a down day, with my thoughts going to Anne and the kids. Home seems a long way away.

Today is also the day to clean out the shitter and replace the bag. Unfortunately a woman from one of the other groups has used it and 'sprayed' everywhere — seriously gross. It was definitely a long stick job and a clean-up of all the snow around as well — I was not a happy chappy.

Phurba and another sherpa arrive and share their brekky with me — a milky rice pudding with cashews that tasted fantastic. Henry Todd, who's the leader of one of the other expeditions, goes by and mentions that the weather window is weakening. Henry specialises in the southern route on Everest, and like Russ brings clients to Cho Oyu to train. Summit day looks to be a few days out, he says — which means I might get to stand on the top on my birthday yet!

Worryingly, my stumps got very cold yesterday when I was out climbing, so today I line the outside of the sockets with another layer of neoprene to be on the safe side. Luckily the stumps warm up very quickly when put in the bivvy boots — a good trick to know. Then it's back up the hill and onto the fixed ropes for the last time before the summit attempt — I have certainly got to know this place well.

24 September

Camp 1 to camp 2 today. The acclimatisation phase is over and it's summit push time. The rest of the team arrived last night so it is an early start and away. The ice cliff traverse is a breeze now that heaps of people have been on it, though there were still other parties jumaring (ascending) up the vertical pitch instead — pretty dumb, and also quite inconsiderate to people wanting to abseil down the lines. Once over the cliff there is a big basin that's hot as hell, with the sun reflecting off all its sides. The route then goes up the steep back wall of the basin, through some crevasses and on up to the next basin where camp 2 is situated.

The fixed ropes start about halfway up the slope out of the first basin and continue winding through the slots — safe as houses but very difficult to use. Unfortunately people coming down in the soft afternoon conditions have made a dog's breakfast of the steps, so if you are a double amputee it makes it really hard to keep your balance. I topped out that slope with very sore stumps. With quite a way still to go to camp 2 memories of Aoraki/Mount Cook in 2001 came flooding back — on that climb I shredded my stumps in similar conditions. Russ relieved me of my pack, and with a bit of stump-socket adjustment it was away again. Now it was a slow, slow trip to the camp, having to stop at least every 20 steps, leaning over the poles so I could catch some breath. Camp 2 kept just out of reach. The last 100 metres seemed to take ages, but then that is what it is like climbing at 7500 metres without supplemental oxygen. Thankfully everyone else looked as shagged as I felt.

When you finally sit down and look out, the view from this camp is awesome. There are towering peaks all around, and while you are higher than most of them the landscape has yet to flatten with the height. It is a very safe camp, nestled in a basin, with no shortage of tents and several other expeditions queued up. Many people are here to celebrate the 50th anniversary of the first ascent of Cho Oyu, while others like me are here for one reason and one reason only — to practise for the big one: Everest.

25 September

Another brilliant day on the hill and only a 'short walk' today, just 400 vertical metres. And they are just about vertical too, up to camp 3 at 7900 metres! The route climbs out of the basin that camp 2 is situated in, rising steeply to a narrow ridge that eventually merges into the rock band below the summit snowfields. Russ's camp 3 is of course the top camp, just 50 or so metres under the rock band. No oxygen today for me, though many on the expedition have plugged in already, using it both to sleep on last night and to climb on today. The air is certainly thin, but I use the sherpa technique of rush and pant, and the climb goes really well. In fact I am the first client to reach camp 3 without using oxygen (yeah, yeah, I know — it helps if you leave first; I do need to be early, hate being late).

Now camp 3 is a different kettle of fish entirely from camp 2. It's perched on some ice ledges cut out of the steep slope, so there is no room to wander around. Anyway, it's summit day tomorrow, so everyone is bunked down early breathing oxygen to help them sleep — everyone except Inglis, that is. I can only afford one bottle of oxygen (at US$400 each) so I save it for the summit day.

26 September

3am and it is time to leave. It is also the time when I realise I have made a huge mistake. The lack of oxygen overnight has meant I have had a long, cold night lying awake listening with envy to Chuck's rhythmic breathing through his mask while I pant in the thin air. What is worse, though, is that at this height oxygen means warmth; it is like the fuel in the fire — no fuel and the fire goes out. The body's periphery shuts down, with the result that at 3am all my fingers, and more worryingly my stumps, are cold, numb and functioning poorly. Well, the stumps aren't so much numb as super-tender, and I have compounded the problem by leaving them in the carbon-fibre sockets all night. This was Mark trying to be smart and get a head start in the morning, always the most difficult time, especially when it is 20°C below zero.

Unfortunately the result was less circulation to the stumps, and I just about froze those puppies right off. I'm probably lucky I didn't give myself frostbite. Add to that a head-lamp that goes flat in the first

Oxygen and altitude — what is it all about?

Although the percentage of oxygen in the air we breathe is constant at different altitudes, the fall in atmospheric pressure at higher altitudes decreases the partial pressure of inspired oxygen, and hence the driving pressure for gas exchange in the lungs. There is a veritable ocean of air present right up to 9000–10,000 metres, where the troposphere ends and the stratosphere begins, but the weight of air above us is responsible for the atmospheric pressure, which is normally about 100 kPa at sea level. Oxygen makes up about 21% of dry air, but as atmospheric pressure and inspired oxygen pressure fall roughly linearly with altitude they end up being about 50% of the sea level value at 5500 metres, and only 30% of the sea level value at 8900 metres (the height of the summit of Everest). The fall in inspired oxygen pressure effectively means there is less oxygen available.

The two significant effects of this are hypoxia (a deficiency in the amount of oxygen reaching the body tissues) and a change in our blood chemistry to counteract the shortfall.

Hypoxia has progressive effects on the functioning of the central nervous system, and it may be that many accidents that occur at extreme altitude on Everest and other mountains are due to poor judgement as a consequence of hypoxic depression of cerebral function. What is more worrying is the fact that these effects on cerebral function may be permanent. The American Medical Research Expedition to Everest studied its climbers a year after their

20 metres (Todd is using my spare one; so much for being prepared) and an oxygen mask that is so bulky I can't see my feet, and you have the makings of a seriously shitty day.

I flop down on my arse and ask Russ what the weather report is like. If it is going to be OK tomorrow then I need to start again fresh, as today isn't going to work. At least I learnt that much on Cook in 2001 — if things aren't right, pull back and make them right, otherwise only disappointment and tears will ensue.

The weather looks as though it will hold, and Russ is willing to let Whetu and two sherpas stay on for a summit attempt tomorrow. The day is spent scavenging all the partly full oxygen bottles that others have discarded and breathing some oxygen, getting some warmth back in

---

return to sea level. They found some enduring abnormalities of cognitive function and ability to perform fast repetitive movements, although most of the functions tested had returned to pre-expedition values.

Initially on travelling to altitude concentrations of blood haemoglobin (our oxygen carrier) rise through a fall in the plasma volume due to dehydration. Later, over a period of five to nine days, hypoxia stimulates production of erythropoietin by the kidneys. This results in an increase in haemoglobin production, and blood haemoglobin concentrations may rise as high as 200 g/l. The increased viscosity of the blood, coupled with increased coagulability, increases the risk of stroke and venous thromboembolism.

Supplemental oxygen is generally used by climbers over 7500 metres. High-pressure, lightweight stainless steel 4 litre bottles, wrapped in carbon fibre for strength, supply pure oxygen through a mask system similar to that worn by pilots; in fact, most common masks are sourced from ex-airforce (Russian) supplies. Oxygen is used to sleep on at rates of 0.5–1 litres per minute, and to climb on at generally 2 litres per minute. On the summit of Everest this would replicate an altitude of about 7500 metres, certainly not sea level. The weight of the cylinders (4–5 kg each) effectively limits the amount any one person can use to what they can carry up high; generally this is two bottles.

the limbs, and generally preparing for tomorrow to make sure it works, unlike today.

27 September

Summit day and also my 45th birthday. 3am seems fine today. I scored my head-lamp back from Todd as he headed down from the summit yesterday, so at least I have light this morning. (Everyone summited, a great result, though there were some pretty shagged people coming by mid-morning as they headed down to as low as they could get, most to camp 1, I think.) Add to that all the work I did on the mask yesterday, stripping it down to the bare minimum so I can see my feet — well, almost anyway (sorry, Russ, just wrecked another bit of your kit) — and we have the makings of a great day.

While I am feeling great today Whetu has picked up a bug that has him vomiting on a regular basis. Does that worry him? Well, probably yes, but he just gets on with the day regardless. Up through the rock band, then it is a long climb up the steep summit snow and ice field. After a few hours of climbing it flattens off to the summit plateau, a huge area the size of several football fields — so where the hell is the real top? Just follow the footprints, and sure enough, just before 8am we come to the streaming prayer flags that mark the summit. The mist is swirling about but you can feel the sun trying to burn through it. I am down to just two layers on top and my down shorts unzipped right up the side, though the sherpas and Whetu are still zipped up in their down suits. I guess I am just a bit weird.

More importantly, I don't need oxygen. I'm standing here on the sixth highest mountain in the world at 8201 metres and I am breathing just fine. I'm not doing any long sprints of course, but I'm pretty comfortable, which is a huge confidence boost when I consider that other hill that is poking through the mist. Yep, Everest, right there. It is only 649 metres higher than where I am standing, though to put Cho Oyu in its rightful place we are still probably 100 metres lower than the top camp, camp 4, on Everest.

While Whetu films I re-duct-tape the legs on in preparation for the long downhill to come, and call home. It's awesome to be able to speak to Anne, and now that she knows I've made it she can relax. Although there

For some reason the officials in Nepal thought this was the first ascent of an 8000 metre peak by a double amputee, but actually the first was my mentor, Norman Croucher of the UK, who summited Cho Oyu in 1995.

With me on the summit were Mark Whetu, Loppsang Temba Sherpa and Karsang Namgel Sherpa.

are a tough few days to come, the worst of the dangerous stuff is over. It's time to head home and prepare for the next one.

Down — the worst thing about climbing mountains is the bloody climb down off them. It's no use moaning, though — just pull finger and get on with it. Whetu puts me on a leash when the slope gets really steep, before we get down to the fixed ropes. I think he has an image of another bolt breaking in the leg and me going flying. Yep, it is tough, but it's good cramponing for a change, which helps heaps. Pretty soon the fixed ropes that lead down through the rock band appear — time for some arm rapping (a bit like abseiling facing out with the rope wrapped once around the forearm, and then running straight down!). Then we are back at camp 4, Cho Oyu done and dusted.

The boys nearly have the camp fully packed up by the time we are ready to move again. They're carrying huge, enormous packs, and they also each have a big bag on a leash like a toboggan. Obviously they would rather put in this one super-effort than climb back up for another load — and even more likely is that Russ, aka Big Boss, has told them this is what they have to do!

It would be nice to get down to camp 1 today but the energy levels and stump health are telling me camp 2 only, thanks. Whetu's load looks as big as the sherpas', hence one very guilty-feeling double amputee carrying a light load, though you'd think I would have got over that sort of stuff by now.

Camp 2 is a godsend, though the last few hundred metres take ages.

Thankfully Loppsang and Karsang come up to help out with our packs after dumping their own loads.

It's amazing how quickly you perk up after a brew and a beer, especially with all of ABC singing 'Happy Birthday' over the radio. What an awesome day! The relief is enormous, though there is still a nervous tingle at the thought of what is to come over the next few tough days.

28, 29 September

The stumble and stagger down to ABC, and then even worse on to base camp, is pretty much as my overactive imagination had anticipated — pretty painful and gross really. About 30 minutes out from ABC things are tender but still going OK, though the concentration required is intense. Phurba and one of the other sherpas come up to meet us. Phurba is carrying climbing rope and some sleeping mats — what for? Well, Big Boss sent him up to carry me down! Piss off! It was very nice to give our packs over to the boys, after explaining to them that while I have legs I walk and if Big Boss wants me carried he will need to steal the legs! Walking into ABC was one of the proudest moments of my life, far more important than climbing Cook. No one can say I didn't do this myself.

Beers and the odd whisky end up being the most effective painkillers that night as we pack up our ABC barrels. There's to be no rest here. The others have had a day off, but my penance for summiting a day late is no rest. We head to base camp to meet up with the jeeps for the trip home tomorrow.

This was the worst day coming up the hill and it's definitely by far the worst going down. Nutrition is based around how many painkillers I can take without damaging myself — a lot, as it turned out. In the usual post-summit rush everyone, including Karsang, rapidly disappears down the glacier, so I spend many hours alone in my own little bit of hell, definitely a stagger and stumble. It doesn't help that I get hopelessly off track (what track?) and end up needing to climb a 100 metre high moraine wall to check out where to go. The last 3 km or so down to the interim teahouse, where I was hoping a truck and the rest of the team would be waiting, was revolting. There are multiple small tears on the skin of the stumps and some pretty major bruising as well, I think. The only way to get through the pain is to power-walk using the poles.

Just get right into it, jog almost, because the quicker it is over with, the quicker it is over with!

Thankfully, I ride the last 10 km to base camp in the relative comfort of the front seat of the truck. As I travel down with Russ, the first topic of discussion isn't the stumps, isn't the summit of Cho Oyu, but simply what do I need to do and what will it cost to nail Everest? Russ reckons it is ten times as hard as Cho — is he just trying to scare me? Perhaps it's better to expect it to be harder than it really will turn out to be. Then, of course, there's the biggie — I will need to effectively pay for an extra sherpa (no problem there) so it will cost US$50,000 — ouch! Russ agrees to hold a place each year from now until the day I can nail the dollars. Look out Everest — I know damn well I can stand on your summit if you let me.

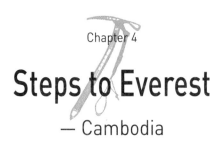

Chapter 4

Steps to Everest

— Cambodia

February 2006 and every day is a day closer to leaving, and just that much more scary! I'm writing this flying home from a week in Rarotonga with Anne — the perfect place to train for Everest! Actually it's the perfect place to escape for a few days' rest before the circus steps up a notch.

So what about the training? Well, it is trucking along really, though I am not working nearly as much on the bike as I had planned. But I am doing heaps of leg and upper-body climbing simulation work in the gym and on the hills around home. Working on strength is critical — one of the lessons I learnt on Cho Oyu is that you can never be too strong. One of the other goals of training is to ensure that every bit of kit is performing as expected, which thanks to the team at Kathmandu it is. I used bivvy booties on Cho Oyu to great effect, as they enabled me to get around without legs on in even the worst situations. I found that the same technique worked on the coral reefs of Rarotonga, using dive booties worn backwards on the stumps instead. Even better, I have come up with a design for closed-cell foam booties for Everest that have the potential to act as 'camp legs' in even the highest camps — a 'great step forward', as they say. Now the challenge is either to find someone to make them for me, or to find the time to do it myself.

Time has really flown since the day in August last year when the dream of having the resources to climb Everest moved to become a reality. In my role as a motivational speaker I presented a talk to the staff of Ahrens Engineering, a family-owned and -run company based in the Barossa Valley of South Australia. I had met the managing director,

Stefan Ahrens, and his wife Leanne at a conference in Auckland just after returning from Cho Oyu. They were planning to get all their staff together in Surfers Paradise to celebrate a great year, and they thought my message on life would be of benefit to them. During a dinner with the family in Surfers the subject of Everest came up, as it always does with me somehow. Some probing questions were asked, not just about how much it would cost, but whether I could really pull it off!

They must have been convinced, because at the company dinner the following evening Stefan stood up in front of his team and announced that Ahrens would be the major sponsor of my Everest expedition. Well, you could have bowled me over with a feather. I was stunned. I immediately got on the phone to Anne, even though it was some ungodly hour back in New Zealand. What a feeling, not just of gratitude, but a huge feeling of responsibility. Here was someone who was going to back me to the tune of US$50,000 to enable me to turn my dream into a reality — and hopefully do some good along the way. Both Ahrens and I wanted more than just a summit to come out of this.

After a discussion with the board of Ahrens, it was decided that we would use the project to raise funds for the Cambodia Trust. This is a trust that provides limbs and prosthetic training not just to the people of Cambodia, but to those of many other poor and war-ravaged countries.

Why that particular charity? Well, I am one of the patrons of the New Zealand branch of the trust, and in 2003 I had the privilege of spending just over two weeks in Cambodia working with amputees and limb fitters. What a great experience that was. I was able to spend several days wandering around the temples of Angkor Wat, one of the wonders of the world, and I also visited the gruesome and moving museums of the killing fields that depict the Pol Pot era. But the real highlight, and my reason for being there in the first place, was working with the very disadvantaged disabled people both in the slums of Phnom Penh and in the paddy fields, jungles and mine-infested countryside they call home.

The Cambodia visit was the brainwave of Ian Kidman, who for the last 15 years or more has been intimately involved with the trust and the people of Cambodia. It was a rare privilege to travel the country with him and see the respect in which he is held, and even more import-antly to see some of the families and kids he has helped over the years.

Cambodian Diary, September 2003

20 September

Singapore. It's 10pm Singapore time, and I'm rattling along the highway in a bus. Eleven hours in the plane, one hour getting through customs etc, then 45 minutes into town on the shuttle bus. Looking out the window at the palm-lined streets and the occasional old building brings visions of the Japanese marching along these streets in the old war movies. I know I should just 'chill' when travelling, and I normally do, but not tonight.

Travel hint #1

If you have a 12-hour layover in Singapore (at night) don't go into town to a hotel unless you are going out on the town for the night or have some other really good reason (I can't think of one at present). Stay out at Changi Airport, do some people-watching, shopping, take the Sky Train tour into the city and back, and get a room at the transit hotel. It will save you perhaps six hours of travel and questions, customs, immigration, airline clerks and all those other wee travel foot-trips that build up to make STRESS.

When I travel I generally just want to get there PDQ. If you must have a layover then make it a few days or a few hours, but don't bugger about with anything in between, honest!

21 September

As the plane climbs up into the smoggy morning air of Singapore, a stunning city is revealed. I would have loved to have seen more of it than the deserted streets at 5am on the way to the airport. Cloud covers the South China Sea and Cambodia, denying me a view until just ten minutes before we land in the northern city of Siem Reap. Then the monsoon cloud clears to reveal images straight out of a Vietnam war movie — gently rolling hills covered in jungle; bloated, brick-red streams and rivers, and small pole-house settlements joined by dirty ribbons of track. Flying today with sophisticated navigation systems you know exactly where you are. Back in the war it's no wonder they bombed every wrong target — or perhaps they just didn't care.

Tonle Sap, a huge freshwater lake that grows during the monsoon to three times its dry-season size, appears through the cloud, and even from 2000 metres up you can see the floating city of the fishing community near Siem Reap.

The first tentative taste of Cambodia comes in the arrival hall. Armed with Ian's advice I have everything ready — application forms, passport photos and US$20, correct change, no big notes. As soon as I walk into the arrival hall three police officers converge on me. They take me to one side and ask for money and documents. Jesus, I think, Cambodian corruption in my first few minutes. But no, it's Cambodian courtesy. They obviously didn't think I should be standing in a line, so they took everything away to the head of the queue and fast-tracked my entry into Cambodia.

As I stepped off the plane the heat and humidity were just a hint of what I would face outside over the next few weeks. Although the arrival hall was not air-conditioned it did have fans that almost interlocked on the ceiling. No such fans outside, just 40 or 50 taxis and motos (small step-through motorcycles), with all the drivers yelling extremely loudly to get your attention and business. What a taste of Cambodia! I must admit you don't see such passion for your business in our one cab back in Hanmer Springs.

I knew the good people at the Cambodia Trust had arranged for someone from the hotel to meet me, so it was a bit like doing a police identity parade as I walked down the line of all these imploring taxi drivers to see the boards they were holding up. Many had people's names on them, most just said 'Hire me', but my guy was the only one not yelling — he was a hotel doorman, far too cultured to join in the frenzy, and anyway, he didn't need to!

Just to digress for a minute — in Cambodia they take the job of door-man very seriously. At the Prum Bayon where I was staying, a good mid-level hotel, the hospitality is traditional Cambodian rather than the more sterile European version. Here the doorman stands by the door with one hand on the handle all the time — I mean all the time. If he needs to leave, it is tag-team time and doorman number 2 takes over — incredible.

The first few hours here confirmed a number of things about the roads:

- there are no road rules other than 'use the horn as much as possible';

- look out for yourself, as no one else will;

- there is obviously no WOF, licence, etc for any vehicle — just drive what you like.

It took me a whole day to realise that they drive on the right here. Most cars are left-hand-drive American 'Japanese' imports — well, about two-thirds are anyway; the balance are right-hand-drive, because it just doesn't seem to matter.

Walking is by far the most difficult way to get around here. Since you are slower than the traffic, getting across the streams of traffic to the other side of the road is the Cambodian version of Russian roulette. Just outside my hotel on NW6 (one of the country's major highways) is the only piece of formed footpath on the whole road. It is about 400 metres long, with a pedestrian crossing at each end, built by the French apparently. The only problem is that no one takes any notice of the zebra crossing and it would be death to any pedestrian if they expected anyone to stop for them!

After walking the streets of Siem Reap in 35°C for the afternoon it's time to get a moto back to the hotel, as tiredness and dehydration are taking hold. What an experience the moto is! To be in that traffic flow and not be at the controls is rather scary for some of us. But having survived that, it is time to think about getting something to eat.

Now negotiating a French menu can be challenging at times — what you think you have ordered and what you actually get can sometimes create a culinary surprise. But wait until you try the same in an authentic Khymer restaurant! Besides the mysteries of the terminology, there were the images of the market that I had just seen. It seems to be cheaper here to wave the flies away than to rely on refrigeration, and the pork (at least I think it was pork) that I saw being cut up looked as if it had been sitting in the sun for a whole week (in New Zealand that is — the equivalent of a few hours in the heat and humidity here).

For dinner I head across the road to the Banteray Sei, recommended in the guide books as a favourite of the local Khymer elite. Well, when in Rome, as they say. Luckily NW6 is a bit quieter than it had been earlier, so it is less of a dash than before. As I enter the semi-outside dining area I get directed to the more casual area where the locals are sitting, rather than the more elegant interior where some westerners are dining at neatly set tables — what's that about? Do I look that rough, or is it the carbon legs perhaps?

The courtyard where I end up is full of Honda Dream motos (quite shiny and looking near-new) and a few Honda CRVs — there's obviously wealth around here somewhere. The temperature is still 30°C+ and 95% humidity at 8pm, so needless to say I am sweltering. It is just so much more difficult for a double amputee to get rid of heat and there are only so many clothes we are allowed to take off!

Anyway, getting back to dinner, as I can't make up my mind I ask the waiter (who has as much English as I have Khymer) for the restaurant speciality. Apparently it is sour beef salad with steamed rice — but what the menu doesn't mention is that it is RAW sour beef salad. With it sitting in front of me all I can think is, well, if you are going to get the shits it'll start right here. I am too chicken — or is that too proud? — to send it back and ask for something cooked, which is fortunate because even with the trepidation of the oncoming shits I get an explosion of flavour that I have rarely ever experienced. I also decide that there is enough chilli in it to kill any bugs — it just about sterilised me as well. No shits follow, which is a serious bonus.

22 September

Angkor Wat day today. According to the guide books it pays to head there at lunchtime if you are travelling alone as all the tour groups will have been herded into the many restaurants, leaving the ruins deserted and allowing you to experience the full power of the place. What they don't mention is that with no one else there you become the sole focus of the many kids who inhabit the ruins looking for handouts and to scam a poor Kiwi double amputee. Mostly they are sent on their way with some fun bantering. I hire one as a guide for a few hours at an hourly rate that even a tradesman back home would smile at, but I also find myself in a position where I am threatened by a group of six or so near the top of one of the ruins. Luckily the threat of taking a leg off and using it to give them a beating has them running away in laughter.

I won't bore you with all the facts and figures about this amazing place — you just need to go there, there is no other way to experience it.

23 September

Another day in Siem Reap. Helicopters Cambodia, which is owned by Helicopters New Zealand, have generously sponsored my flights here, and their pilot, Andrew, has organised a look through the Halo Trust headquarters. The trust, which has its National HQ here in Siem Reap, runs worldwide humanitarian mine-clearing operations. Here in Cambodia is apparently one of the better postings for an ex-pat, of which they have three. They are all based here in Siem Reap, but travel the country extensively. Considering their job it's hard to imagine worse postings, but 'Suds', a recent team member, thinks he's pretty lucky to be here. His previous postings were Eritrea and Caucasia, with a stint in Bosnia, all far more remote with little other ex-pat contact. Here they have a sizeable town (Siem Reap) with about 150 other ex-pats, most of whom can be found at about five bars on any given night.

In Cambodia the Halo Trust employs over a thousand staff, all Cambodian apart from those three ex-pats, and trained in the sophisticated procedures of mine clearing by the Halo staff. The task is huge. In just one small minefield last week (one of hundreds) they were averaging 192 mines per hour. That's just detecting them — then they have to explode them in situ. It is a huge credit to their systems that they have very few injuries to their staff. The most recent was a Land Rover rolling — better and more preventable than a mine blowing up in your face.

Travel and intelligence about the minefields are some of their biggest hurdles. They spend a lot of time researching the potential known minefields, using local knowledge, looking for evidence of mines such as animal and human remains, or blown-up vehicles, plus any military-derived information. From this bank of data they draw maps and decide the priority for clearance, as just because there is a minefield somewhere doesn't mean they have the resources to clear it. The main priorities hinge around the current danger to the locals, and then the likely use that will be made of the cleared land.

After a very sobering visit to the Halo Trust Andrew treats me to a flight in his Squirrel over Angkor Wat. This is a great way to appreciate the scope of the place. There was some serious engineering done down there over several hundred years to create the temples, canals and water-storage reservoirs, which are the size of small lakes.

The afternoon is spent with Mr Serey, my moto driver, on a trip out to the floating villages. Once there I hire a longboat to take me right out through the waterways to the lake itself. It's amazing to see this community of people who live their whole lives on the water, as do their animals. There are floating pig and chicken cages, farmed alligators and fish, even floating hospitals, police stations and schools. As always I get told off for taking photos of the police station; Mr Serey says, 'Bad people, no photo,' and in this case I am more than happy to take his advice.

24 September
Still in Siem Reap. The first few hours of the morning are spent catching up with emails and business, then writing my speech for the 1 October graduation ceremony so it can be translated. It's one of the very few times I have ever written a speech down. It is timed for five minutes, though it's

bloody hard to get me to shut up after only five minutes, I can assure you.

Mr Serey and I go for a look around Siem Reap for a few hours, calling in at the icons of the town — well actually just some of the interesting buildings and bars, plus a few bookstores as well. You can tell the ex-pats in town as they either drive 4WDs or more commonly a decent trail bike (mostly Honda XRs).

There are probably 10 to 15 amputees and other disabled people begging in the old market, along with kids with babies, and other adults, a sight you unfortunately get very used to here.

I'm definitely getting the hang of the currency now, though there is no way I am as sharp as the dumbest Cambodian — these guys are born entrepreneurs and con artists. There's 4000 riel to the US dollar, so that means 50 cents = 2000 riel, which you generally get in two 1000-riel notes. The notes seem to be either brand new (probably counterfeit) or disgustingly grubby. I'm sure if you got sick here it would be from handling the money — it really does look like they wiped their backside with it sometimes. No wonder you don't see any loo paper anywhere!

It has just occurred to me that during yesterday's flight we saw 500 metres in every direction and nowhere in sight were there any sewerage ponds — I guess it all goes into the streams, lakes and paddy fields.

25 September
Today I fly to Phnom Penh, down the length of the Tonle Sap to where its outfall, which is also its intake, joins with the mighty Mekong. For the next eight days I will be staying in Phnom Penh each night (just down from the Foreign Correspondents Club) and each day heading out into the hinterland to meet with amputees and other disabled people. My aim is to show them what is possible, though I guess even I haven't come within a cooee of that yet. Ian is my host here, and, along with our driver Horn (sorry if I have misspelt your name), we go exploring in the Land Cruiser each day.

27 September
Another birthday away from home. It is getting to be an unfortunate habit really. It also rubs in how much I miss the family. I wish Anne and the kids were here to experience Cambodia. It is an amazing mix, a city and country of contrasts — the aromas from spices to marijuana to sewage to blossoms (and that is only in 50 metres); from the tragedy of the killing fields to the beauty of the people. No wonder Ian has been coming here

for so long. The other thing here is that such a small amount of resources can go so far — a US dollar is a powerful tool. You can feed a family for a year on just a few hundred dollars and educate their kids for even less — Ian does.

I visit the Veterans International facility to see some of the great work they do there (like the Cambodia Trust they create limbs, but also specialise in components such as handmade feet and a variety of wheelchairs and hand bikes). While I'm there I meet the very successful Cambodian disabled volleyball team, all amputees, sponsored by the large international prosthetics company, Otto Bock. They're a group of passionate athletes who now have a new lease on life — great to see.

30 September
A day out at Kampong Chnnang limb centre today, about 90 minutes north of Phnom Penh on the shores of the Tonle Sap. Interestingly, a limb centre anywhere in the world is a limb centre — any amputee feels at home. This is my first chance to see the legs, arms and orthotics being made up close. The legs are made almost identically to mine at home, probably because most of the tutors have been Kiwis and Aussies. There is one main difference, though; because of the tough climatic conditions they don't use resins and glass or carbon fibre, but sheets of a polyester-type material that is heat-formed over the stump socket moulds — very smart.

We have lunch at a riverside restaurant that is my undoing. Each day I have emailed home 'no shits today!' but no more. I only just made it back into the hotel in the evening before both ends let go; add to that a raging fever and I feel near death. I lie on the bathroom floor with my cheek against the nice cool porcelain of the loo bowl for hours on end. Sportsmed in Christchurch kitted me out with some great new antibiotics for just such an eventuality; the only trouble is keeping a pill down long enough for it to do some good. Now I know everyone gets ill occasionally, and it normally passes after a few days, but that's no use to me. Tomorrow, 1 October, is the whole reason I am here — the graduation ceremony for the latest batch of prosthetists — so I need to be upright, with a tight, reliable anal sphincter!

1 October
Well, things are very delicate, but I think I can manage with a bit of careful planning — like knowing exactly where a loo is at any time, in any place, and having the fastest possible route to it planned.

In the end things work out well, though after 11 days or so of dealing with extreme poverty I really am a bit povertied out. To my rescue comes Kevin, the country manager for Helicopters Cambodia, who takes me out for a meal and a beer to meet some of the ex-pats working in Cambodia. That really has given me far more faith in what is achievable here once the government can win the battle with the extreme corruption rife here.

To help get the message of the charity out there I have created a website, www.legsoneverest.com. The idea is that either Anne or I will update it, so people can follow the adventure and have the opportunity to donate desperately needed funds that will go directly to the Cambodia Trust. What would we do without Tracey Richardson's 'fundraise online' facility — it has never been easier to set up a transparent way of directing funds to your chosen charity.

The media has become very interested in the adventure — a wee bit too interested for my liking, but that's life. There is a significant article in *North and South* magazine, but no, Anne and I aren't going to be on the cover of the *Woman's Weekly*! The radio stations MoreFM, VivaFM and SoundsFM have all been very active and supportive, as has Radio New Zealand. In the UK, the *Daily Telegraph* has run an article, as has their stablemate the *South China Morning Post*. In Australia, the *Sydney Morning Herald* has done a page-six slot, and there have been radio slots with 3AW Melbourne, 2YE Sydney and an FM station in Sydney, all very positive and hopefully raising awareness of the Cambodia Trust.

The next month is taken up with travelling the length and breadth of New Zealand, motivating groups — or at least that is the general idea. The training steps up a notch or two both in the gym and on the bike (thanks to Sheppard Industries I have an extremely sexy new lime-green Specialized Epic Comp bike, a seriously awesome ride). It's also a busy time with my new sportsfood brand, PeakFuel, which is sponsoring several events and undergoing major growth. All this combines to keep us well and truly on our toes!

PeakFuel — now there is one of my new passions. After years as a winemaker and an athlete I couldn't face any more of those tasteless, or worse, noxious-tasting, sportsfoods out there. So what to do? Make your own — that is what. I have designed four gels and packaged them in what I think is more responsible packaging — a toothpaste tube! Add to that two electrolyte drinks and all of a sudden my business partners, Norm and Lorraine Wilson, have become sportsfood producers! So to add to the guilt of being away from the family for three months or so I am also having to shoulder Norm, Lorraine and Anne with my share of the PeakFuel workload. At least I will be testing the product in one of the hardest environments on earth — the roof of the world!

Like most things in life, while I love doing things myself, PeakFuel was, without help, always going to be a dream (sounds familiar, doesn't it?). And that is where Norm and Lorraine stepped into the breach. After a chance meeting in Blenheim in early 2005 they came on board to help provide some oomph to everything, and they have been invaluable ever since. The one thing I can be sure about is that after Everest the next big challenge in life will be to make sure PeakFuel becomes an international success — nothing like stating your aims to make you follow through!

25 March 2006

A Saturday morning at Christchurch Airport. The plane leaves in 30 minutes, and it is time to go through security. How come every time I want to hug the family and say goodbye there is a camera in our faces? We have brought it on ourselves, I guess, so we just have to grin and bear it. Anne's mum, dad and brothers are here for a while, and most importantly Anne and our daughter Amanda. The tears of emotion are very difficult to control as I go through the security gate. But every time you step on the plane there is that feeling of release; you're on the way to another adventure.

Over the last two days I have been in Dunedin, Ashburton, home in Hanmer Springs and back to Christchurch — just an average few days really. Two talks in one day, 400-plus km apart, are no problem, especially as the client in Ashburton generously allowed my mum to come along. After almost three years of my motivational speaking, Mum had never been to an event. Driving from Dunedin to Ashburton meant I could pop through Geraldine and pick Mum up, and even better head back to Geraldine to spend the night. Without Mum and Dad's support I would never have been able to turn my hobby, climbing, into my life — not that Mum is necessarily too keen on the idea even now. I must admit it took me a wee while to get up the courage to admit to her that Everest was a reality! The poor lady has had to put up with 46 years of my escapades so far, and unfortunately for her they are unlikely to diminish in the next few years.

Chapter 5

On the way to Kathmandu

— gateway to Everest

26 March

Bangkok

Once again it's 31° and high humidity, and here I am with my bags full of winter gear! I take a taxi ride to the centre of town and I am back at the Indra Regent Hotel; it really is nice when the staff remember you. Now if I was a cynical sod I would say that they have a pat line that they give to everyone, but perhaps I shouldn't be so cynical as they commented that I had less luggage this time!

As always it was hectic in the build-up to leaving New Zealand, and hard leaving the family in Christchurch and the team that turned out at Auckland Airport to make sure I left the country (thanks Robyn, Dave, Hannah, Moose and family, Chas and Di). The week Anne and I had in Rarotonga was a godsend. It's the first time I have really enjoyed the islands, and what's more I felt only mildly guilty when I resurfaced in New Zealand. More importantly, it gave us some essential relaxation time and a break from the frenetic activity of the last few months.

Thai Airlines now has a direct flight from Auckland to Bangkok, and it's one of the new Airbus planes as well — a great relief after the last trip in the old MD11 bucket. A truly relaxing 13 hours or so in the air. It's my longest period away from email in months, and an even bigger shock is that I have left my laptop at home for Anne to manage — that is unheard of for me. Yep, it's internet cafes in Nepal and Tibet, and Russ's guaranteed bullet-proof satellite broadband at base camp and advanced base camp — they had bloody better be!

After a few hours' sleep the body clock is well on the way to changing. That's the reason for spending a day here — going from New Zealand to Bangkok involves the biggest time change of the trip. This is a good place to adjust, to 'chill' out (not likely) and get your head out of home mode and into expedition mode. Whetu suggested having a day in Bangkok en route to Cho Oyu, not just as a means of getting the body clock adjusted, but perhaps more importantly, to get the head away from the inevitable rush of getting away so you can step into climbing mode when you land in Kathmandu. Since that first time I have added another 12 hours to the visit (more time to hunt out great food) and it works even better.

By 7am I'm walking about the city. The streets are just awakening and as the only tourist out and about (and also the only double amputee) I get constantly hit on — come on, where are the others?

I need to buy a new camera, either here or in Kathmandu, so I'll need to see what deals are around. Add two SD memory cards to the list, a solar panel, and the chance to eat some great Thai food and it will be a full day! Back to the airport (yet another one) tomorrow at 6am, and on to meet the team.

Twelve hours of wandering the streets of Bangkok is enough. It's 7pm and I'm hungry for some simple, sterile, boring food, or at least some choice. Here it is all street food, which smells fantastic, and I'm sure tastes fantastic, but it's too early in the trip to take the risk! Needless to say the charm of Bangkok has worn off. There are just so many times you can brightly say no to taxis, tuk-tuks and the driver's sister! The TV here is abysmal by our (my?) standards and I have just finished my book, hence the need to write — I must be bored.

It's time to set the alarm and practise waiting. I'll be doing enough of that soon — there are two months of waiting ahead, every day of it as important as the day to the top!

27 March

I couldn't sleep, no way — tossing and turning, too hot without the air-con on, too noisy with it on. I'd like to think it was jet-lag, but I'm sure it was nerves. So I'm up at 5am, pack my bags and check out. I have a car booked for 7am but I really don't want to wait that long, as I explain to the 'lovely' old lady down at the travel desk. After she had reamed me out about not giving enough notice I indicated where she could put her car (with a healthy dose of humour and respect, honest) and told her I would just take a taxi, thanks. Amazingly, the car turned up straight away! I had one of those hard choices at the airport — pay excess baggage and stay in Economy, or upgrade to Business and have no baggage fee — um, let me see, have a guess! Very nice flight, thanks.

Through the haze of the ever-present fires the Himalayan giants showed their shoulders — a nice bit of prose that, don't you think? The trouble is, no matter how tongue-in-cheek you try to be, you can't help being impressed. It's one of the most magical flights around, the equal of which I am sure can only be found above the other great mountain ranges of the world, like at home.

Stepping out of the airport at Kathmandu feels like coming home — the frantic activity at the arrivals gate, and all the trekking and expedition outfits there to collect their charges. Smoky, dusty, clogged streets — Kathmandu hasn't changed. We are staying at the same hotel as on the Cho Oyu trip, the Hotel Tibet, which is tucked away in the Lazimpat district about 20 minutes' walk from central Thamel. I think this is Russ's second home — either here or the Red Onion bar next door! Tsering and her team at the hotel greet us like family. The current guests are mainly our team and an Adventure Consultants (AC) expedition. It's great to catch up with old friends from Cho Oyu like Deano (who has crossed to the 'dark side', we joke, now working for AC rather than Russ); Guy Cotter, the leader/owner of AC, and Russ's Kathmandu staff, led by Chundlim. Then it's time for a quick walk around the streets, catching up with some of the stall-holders and making promises to buy later, when I come back — like all good businessmen they want me to buy now, in case I don't come back!

This is a different Kathmandu though. It's quieter, the tourists still haven't come back after the start of the Maoists' terror programme. In fact tourism, Nepal's most important 'product', is down 50%, and it's even quieter than in 2004.

The difference between Bangkok and here? Well, there isn't the aggressive selling here, but there are the smiles and good-natured bartering. It's so refreshing not to be constantly hit on, though once they get you into the shop you'll be bloody lucky to get out without your wallet being lighter. It's strange really. On a large scale, Kathmandu is much poorer than Bangkok and other Asian cities, it's full of swirling dust (aerosol faeces, actually!) and there's hardly a finished building in sight. But on the human, micro scale it is infinitely cleaner in every sense of the word. Why? Easy — the people. The stall-holders and shopkeepers are constantly sweeping their part of the pavement, keeping things tidy. Some of these shops haven't had a sale in several days, which makes a bit of a mockery of the few tourists trying to barter down to the last rupee — just give them the dosh!

I just about had a tear in my eye as I came down the alley (they call it a street) towards the Hotel Tibet, past the small shopkeepers and the Red Onion bar. Things obviously don't change too much here, as at least half the street call out my name — I obviously spent too much here last time!

It is so easy to get around Kathmandu. It's nothing here to grab one of the wee Suzuki Alto cabs, do a deal for a fare and be confident the only ride you get taken on is to where you need to go! And unlike Bangkok, the drivers aren't so keen to sell their sisters! (No, I didn't ask.) The catch is that there seem to be no particular road rules — the pushiest vehicle wins — so you're safer climbing than riding in cabs.

I grabbed a cab to New Road, doing a deal with the driver so that for 200 rupees he would take me there, wait, and get me back to wherever I wanted to go — I probably paid 100 rupees too much, but what the hell. New Road is the retail area that specialises in electronics at one end, jewellery at the other. It does have a real name but I certainly can't pronounce it, let alone spell it. I need to hunt out a new digital camera that uses both an SD card and AA batteries for power. I have my eye on a wee Nikon that I saw in New Zealand. I found it after about ten shops — yep, that's ten sets of staff determined to do you a deal or to talk you into a better model! In fact, I ended up paying about the same price as the one I didn't buy in Dunedin last week! Who said New Zealand doesn't have great deals. It's a pity I was a bit slow in taking this one up. (Sorry to the salesman at Bond & Bond in Dunedin; you should have got the sale, mate.)

I feel a Red Onion night coming on. It's time to catch up, tell some tall stories (lubricated with the odd G&T), then away into Thamel for dinner. Tradition dictates taking a cab in, rickshaw races home.

28 March

Time for some work for a change. Russ and I travel over to the office of Mountain Experience (the trekking arm of the business)/Himalayan Experience, a multi-storey house out in the 'suburbs'. The idea is to sit down and discuss the plan for Everest, and air our thoughts and concerns. The walls of the office are plastered with images and posters of climbers summiting. There's a fantastic one of Sue Fear on Everest — jeez, I hope I can come home with a piece of memorabilia like that. Much of the discussion involves Russ reminding me how hard it's going to be — thanks, Russ. I still don't resolve all the issues that are concerning me — for example, I have paid a premium (an extra US$10,000) to ensure I have the resources I need on the mountain, but it seems from our talk that I'll get the same as everyone else. How does that work?

It's good to catch up with some of the sherpas, like Lachhu, though some of the team are already on Everest. In fact the sherpas already have base camp (BC) and advanced base camp (ABC) in place, and are hopefully heading to the North Col today, weather permitting. This year Russ has the team in very early to fix ropes that we can trust. In fact, he plans to fix the whole mountain and then try to recoup the significant cost (over 5000 metres — 5 km — of rope!) from the other teams on the hill this year. In previous years this has been done in a pretty haphazard way; this year Russ really will 'own' the mountain.

I'm pretty tired today (perhaps something to do with last night?) but the body clock has adjusted. Now it's time to get the lungs going! I wish I could jump on a plane to Lhasa today, or perhaps a jeep to Kodari, Zhangmu and base camp. What I need now is patience, which is not one of my strengths.

As I sit here in the shade at Hotel Tibet writing I can hear one of the many protest rallies that have been taking place. There's lots of shouting, chanting and drums — the place has a very tense atmosphere at present. Everywhere there are armed soldiers — far more and in more places than in 2004 — hiding behind their sandbagged posts or wandering the streets. Only about half of them are armed, and there is a huge variety of guns from modern infantry rifles to shotguns and old bolt-action rifles. Some are just carrying sticks!

I see in the papers that the Maoist rebels bombed a polytech here yesterday while exams were happening. Luckily no one was injured, but plenty of people got the message. There was hope that the king would provide some leadership and real political strength, but that is looking less and less likely, according to Tsering and other locals. Selfishly, I can't help thinking, 'Just as long as they don't close the border until after the 1st of April.' There are shades here of the 2004 Cho Oyu trip — we got out the day before the border closed then, and Grania and the Prince got stuck for two weeks on the other side.

The hotel staff are flitting around nervously. Fewer rallies, more tourists is what they need. Back in 2004, I read that tourism had dropped 47% since 1999; I am told that today the figure is nearer 85%.

30 March

6.30am — another crisp, clear morning in Kathmandu. Well, at the moment anyway; it's sure to deteriorate to the usual smog later in the day. I just wish my thinking was as crisp and clear as the weather. It was the expedition dinner last night, and though I didn't play up it was a late night all the same — 1am is far too late for an old bugger like me. I escaped 'Tom and Jerry's' relatively early — luckily, by the sound of it, as the bar stays open as long as there are customers. Which can be pretty damned late — or early, depending on how you look at it. Somewhat surprisingly, there are only three of us down for breakfast — I can't imagine why the others aren't up and about!

Today my roommate, Mogens, arrives. No more luxury of a room to myself until we get to base camp in seven days' time. I pity the poor lad really — I hope he has some ear plugs!

I'm feeling very nervous — a combination of Kathmandu fever and the worry that so many of the other members of the team have been out acclimatising in the Khumbu. Whetu, Mogens, Big Tim and some of the others have all been out there, and Whetu has already been to 5600 metres! I've only been up the stairs to the Red Onion bar.

Kathmandu is at 1200 metres, which is hardly high enough to get a decent puff going. Lhasa, where we head next, is at 3600 metres, the same height as Mount Cook, and if my memory serves me right that's enough to give you a spinning head when you arrive. It will be interesting to see how useful my hypoxic training at home has been — I'm sure it's not as good as a week in the Khumbu. I'm seriously thinking that I should have jumped on a plane to Lukla, even just for the night, but it's too late now. Russ says the sherpas have already been to the North Col. It is likely that with good weather some of them might even get the chance to summit by the time we get to ABC, and I must admit to a significant lump of jealousy!

Himalayan Experience 2006 Everest Expedition, and associated Discovery Channel Documentary Expedition

As well as the usual guides, sherpas and climbers, we were accompanied by a film crew, as Discovery Channel was making a documentary about Russ's expedition. The aim was to try to portray what Everest is really like (and hopefully dispel the idea that it is becoming a rich man's playground). Looking at the people on our expedition, it will hopefully show passionate, committed people doing what they love.

The guides
Russell Brice, aka Russ or Big Boss (expedition leader, a Kiwi,
     but lives in France)
William Crouse ('Bill', from the US, head guide)
Shaun Hutson (UK)
Mark Woodward ('Woody', Kiwi)

The climbers
Wayne Alexander ('Cowboy', a Kiwi engineer, and my leg man)
Gerard Bourrat (French)
Maxine Chaya ('Max', Lebanese)
Mogens Jensen (Danish super-hero)
Robert Killup ('Bob', an Aussie)
Brett Merrell (from LA, a fireman)
Terry O'Connor (US, our doctor)
Tim Smith (from the Discovery Channel series *American Chopper*;
     US through and through. Tim is a last-minute addition to the team.

He had been going to climb from the south but decided his chances would be much better approaching from the north with Russ. Tim has a fused ankle which, like my carbon legs, will add to the challenge.)

Mark Inglis (on this trip dubbed 'The Penguin', a Kiwi of course)

Marcel Bach (Swiss)

Kurt Hefti (Swiss; Marcel and Kurt will train in Nepal and join the expedition only once we are at ABC)

The camera crew

Mark Whetu ('Whetu', Kiwi, mountain guide and high-altitude camera operator)

Ken Sauls (US, mountain guide and high-altitude camera operator)

Jen Peedom (Aussie, camera operator)

Dick Colthurst (the film crew boss, UK, producer)

Doug Allan (UK, camera operator)

Colin Bowes (UK, soundy)

Graham Hoyland (UK, producer)

Martin Pailthorpe (UK, producer)

James Drake-Brockman ('Jake', UK, soundy)

Barnabas Revill ('Barney', UK, producer)

Simon Wagen ('Si', UK, Beta camera operator)

Edmund Wardle ('Ed', UK, camera operator)

Stephen White ('Steve', UK, editor)

Sybilla Wilson ('Sybs', UK, production coordinator)

Mark Rogers ('Dodgy', Aussie, stills photographer)

Lisa Walters (UK, production manager)

Everest traverse team

Julien Gustav ('Mario', Swiss, mountain guide)

Dangima Sherpa (Nepali, guide)

Mario is planning on being the first person to climb up from the south and descend by the northern route — the first 'grand traverse' of the mountain — hence he will need to use some of our camps high on the mountain on the way down.

North Col trekking clients

Rosemary Mould (UK)

Gerrit Van Dam (Dutch)

Catharina Voorbrood (Dutch)

ABC trekking client
Irene Kennedy (UK)
It is becoming more common for people who want to experience Everest
but don't want the commitment of summit day (just yet) to use the
infrastructure of the expedition to get up to the North Col or, like
Irene, to advanced base camp. Both places are a real challenge in
themselves.

Most importantly, the sherpas
Nepali, guides
  Phurba Tashi Sherpa
  Son Dorjee Sherpa
  Lhakpa Nuru Sherpa
  Tuk Bahadur Thapa Magar
  Phura Nuru Sherpa
  Loppsang Temba Sherpa
  Karsang Namgel Sherpa
  Dorji Sonam Gyalgen Sherpa
  Pema Chhosang Sherpa
  Ngawang Nurbu Sherpa
Nepali, cooks
  Lachhu Bahadur Basnet
  Rames Kumar Basnet
  Phurba Gharti Bhote
  Phuru Galzen Sherpa
  Danuru Sherpa
  Kul Bahadur Magar
Plus another ten or so Tibetan sherpas, if only I could spell their names!

I'm beginning to appreciate that there are some great people on this
trip. Bill, the head guide, is certainly a powerful-looking guy, with an
extremely laid-back attitude that oozes competence. Shaun, another
guide, works for Russ in Chamonix. He is on his first full Everest trip,
but he's also someone who doesn't need to shout to show he knows what
he's doing.

It's now gear-check time, and the guides and Russ are looking over
our down kit. Both Cowboy and I have had gear made in Christchurch.
I have made use of my experience on Cho Oyu, and Cowboy has used

Which side?

When you think Everest, especially as a Kiwi, you think Sir Ed, Tenzing, Nepal and of course the South Col route they pioneered, including the infamous 'Hillary Step' on the summit ridge. The northern route is less well-known — the approach from Tibet to the north and northeast ridges that run on the left flank of the giant North Face of Everest. This is the route of the 1920s expeditions, like that of Mallory and Irvine, whose bodies still lie on the slopes of the North Face.

So why is the northern route the route of choice for a double amputee? Well, it isn't because it is easier — in fact some say it is more difficult, especially the last day to the summit — but there were several compelling reasons that drove me there:

- It's the route of choice of Russell Brice and his Himalayan Experience expeditions, arguably the most successful outfit on the mountain, and certainly my first choice.

- The ability to drive to base camp — now that has to be good for a double amputee. Let me climb any day, but walk — no thanks! If you take the southern route you have to make a nine-day trek up through the foothills of the Himalayan giants, through the Khumbu region (great for acclimatising, but not for me). This is the home of the Nepalese Sherpa people, and when people think of Nepal, this is usually the area they imagine.

- The biggie — the northern route has no icefall to negotiate. One of the characteristics of the southern route, and possibly its most challenging aspect, is the icefall you have to climb through. Think of a glacier as a river of ice, and an icefall as its steepest rapids — broken blocks of ice the size of houses moving metres every day — a recipe for getting clobbered for sure. Not so many people die in the icefall these days but they still do die there, and it's not a matter of competence, just a case of being in the wrong place at the wrong time.

So all up, for me there is no choice — the north it is. The last day, summit day, has three rock steps that must be climbed, but I reckon I can do it — if I can't then it's nobody's fault but mine.

the same makers. Kathmandu, the outdoor outfitters, supplied all my kit and commissioned my down jacket and shorts, very specialised bits of kit. Knowing how I performed on Cho Oyu I had faith that my gear was plenty warm enough, but Cowboy's was deemed BC/ABC clothing only, so he will be wearing one of Russ's sherpa suits above the North Col. Russ has a rule that no one goes above the North Col without wearing their down suit — no exceptions. Why? The weather changes so quickly and to such an extreme extent that there is no way you can get the suit on part-way up the slope to camp 2. It's hard to imagine here in Kathmandu, but I guess we'll be finding out soon enough!

31 March

At last, the final day in Kathmandu — about time. I think I made a mistake coming so early. Two days would have been heaps of time here. Never mind, let's get the show on the road. Mogens is a great roommate, though the sight of him in his boxers made me feel hugely inadequate. He has the body of a Greek god and must have an incredible power-to-weight ratio. There's not an ounce of fat on him, which is damned lucky as he is planning on riding his bike from here to base camp over five days — it's all uphill, and what a hill! The gorge up to Nylam in Tibet must be 2500 metres of climbing on a rough road — actually it's more like a track, or at least it was back in 2004. I had always thought that to ride a mountain bike down the gorge would be awesome, but to ride one up would be stupendous — if you could do it, that is! It makes the Tour de France look like a Sunday afternoon outing. To complicate matters, Mogens is also an asthmatic. And I thought I took on big projects — they're nothing to what he is going to attempt.

Another traditional expedition evening last night — a meet-and-greet for the climbing and film teams, aka a piss-up. Needless to say, people were feeling a bit delicate today. Bob and Jen have been hit by a similar bug — both ends going, chills and shakes, poor buggers. But perhaps it's better to get nailed by it now rather than halfway across Tibet. At least here there's a real loo, with nice, clean, cool porcelain to rest your cheek against while you wonder which end will go next.

Tsering has arranged for me to visit a spinal rehabilitation unit based out on the same grounds as the country's limb centre and new orthopaedic hospital. Cowboy and I discover pretty much what we expected — it's very tough being a paraplegic or quadraplegic here. The centre is funded by charity (which is typical of all the poorer countries) and deals mostly with the poor from all over Nepal. In many ways it's like Cambodia, but instead of having a disproportionately large number of amputees (because of the landmines, polio and the step-through motos) Nepal has a very high incidence of spinal injuries. Why? It's simple — they fall out of trees a lot! I'm not kidding — a lot of forage harvesting is done up in the trees and there are no OSH safeguards here. Most work practices (and travel) are not controlled and are very dangerous.

Visiting the centre was a pretty moving experience. They're great people in a tough situation. They seemed to enjoy the chat we had — I talked for about 20 minutes (with an interpreter, of course), did the usual leg thing (popped one off for them) and we had a good laugh, something I think they have little of. I commented to Cowboy that despite the different environment it was very similar to the spinal unit at Burwood in Christchurch, where I have spent some time. The challenges facing each of the patients are the same regardless of the country; they are so huge that they transcend the nature of the country and its intrinsic hardships, although the challenges facing the staff are possibly even greater here.

We spied a photo on the wall of Sir Ed opening the unit — it's hard to go anywhere in this city without seeing an image of Ed; I reckon he gives royalty a run for the number of images on show! They have put about 280 patients through the unit so far. Each one costs US$200 a month, with an average stay of three months. It's quite a short time to rehabilitate from a spinal injury, especially when you are going back to a hill village with little in the way of support. Much like the limb centres in Cambodia, each patient (I guess they'd be called 'clients' in New Zealand) has to have a live-in family caregiver. There are two reasons for this: one, there just aren't the staff to go around, and two, to train the family to help once they make it home.

The real tragedy is that 70% of the people who come through here are young women, since they're the ones doing the work in the trees. The reason it's a tragedy is that it's tough to convince many of the families to give them the care they need. I'll go back to the unit on the way home if I can, regardless of the outcome of the climb, and I will probably donate at least one new wheelchair or commit to donating a hand bike. If I don't have time I'll have to get Russ, Chundlim or Tsering to arrange it.

It is frustrating not to have enough time, energy and money to do more for so many deserving people. If you want to help, email them at spinal@wlink.com.np. Just like our Cambodian charity, a little bit goes a long way.

Right next door to the rehabilitation unit is the limb centre, so it would be rude not to pop in and say 'Hi'. It's as quiet as a church in there, with not an amputee in sight, but one look in the workshop and you feel pretty much at home — limb centres anywhere in the world are alike. There are several limb-fitters around, and talk about dead keen to copy the pattern of my leather cuffs (the straps that hold the legs on) — they had a pattern made before you could blink. Again, I will drop in on the way home and leave them all my spare kit — socks, cuffs and my spare foot. I am sure there is a young amputee out there who needs a flexfoot.

Saga, our guide, then takes us through some alleys full of the aromas of back-street Nepal, through a particularly revolting loo area and adjacent kitchen, eventually ending up at the front of the new Nepal Orthopedic Hospital. This is a fascinating place, and we meet Dr Pierre Soete, a consultant from Belgium who's also a mountaineer, as it turns out. He has summited Ama Dablam via the east ridge, which is a serious climb, and attempted the Hornbein Couloir on Everest, another very serious route.

The hospital was established with funding from Rotary International about five years ago and to start with relied on charity for 80% of its funding. Now it's only 10% funded by charity, which is just about the opposite of the trend in most of these places. They have done it by building a state-of-the-art private clinic that charges 1500 rupees a night (US$20) for a luxury room, which subsidises the poor, who pay only 100 rupees in the ward downstairs — a very smart idea.

Yet another team dinner tonight, this time at Kilroys, so another late night! I'll be bloody glad to get to Tibet.

1 April

April Fool's Day. Even smoggier than before. We're up at 5.30am, have a quick breakfast, and are on the bus for the airport. The Adventure

Consultants team is also heading off, so there are goodbyes to the team, and 'Good lucks', especially to Deano. They fly to Lukla and then have a nine-day walk to base camp in preparation for a summit attempt via the South Col. You never know, we might meet on the top! I'd better be careful though; the last time I said that it was to Whetu, on 14 November 1982 — he didn't make it and I got stuck there for over 13 days, so best we don't do that again.

As always in airports in this part of the world, there's lots of hurrying followed by even more waiting around. This time we have four hours of queueing, making sure we're in the same order as on our permits (like little kids, we need to remember the person in front of us, which is a tough job this morning for some), then lots of forms, and even more waiting.

But what a flight! It took ages to climb up through Kathmandu's smog, and out towards the big peaks there was a massive bank of cotton-wool-like cloud. The higher we went the more of the big buggers poked their heads out. Then sliding past the window was Cho Oyu, with just a small cap of cloud on the top. It was great to see it again, especially as last time I was on the top of it looking back this way. And who could mistake Everest — well actually, several people around us are doing 'What mountain is that?' impressions. It really does look bloody mean — windswept, steep, exposed. We are looking directly into the Western Cwm and at the South Col — crikey, the southeast ridge looks steep from here. It's lucky I can't see our route otherwise I'd be even more gripped.

As Everest disappears past the window the high plateau of Tibet is laid out in front of us — brown and tan hills, blue braided rivers, skiffs of snow on the ridges — what an awesome place. Effectively we are flying over the route that we will drive back on in just a few days, over 5300 metre passes to the northern base of Everest. Right now that's quite a scary thought.

Chapter 6

Across the Tibetan plateau

As soon as you step off the plane at Lhasa International Airport you can feel the crisp, clean but thin air. I know it sounds geekish but I was watching my altimetre on the flight in, and the cabin pressure was the equivalent of 2400 metres or so. That's the international standard, but we were flying into an airport at 3700 metres. When that door opens the altitude will instantly be 1300 metres higher — how will that feel? But no, smart people, they manage the cabin pressure over the last 15 minutes of the flight, lowering it to the correct altitude. By the time we land they have taken it from 2400 metres to 3600 metres — damned smart really.

The new airport is a classic big Chinese statement — all glass, granite and marble. They even have air-bridges now! No more bussing over to a stinky old hut. Now it's straight into a huge, cold, echoing, impersonal barn. More queues (yes, in order again) and forms. They even have an infra-red temperature-recording 'gate'; my temperature was 36.8°C, apparently.

The biggest surprises are how cleaned up the local village is, and the beautiful new road, a perfect black-top. Then there's the trip to Lhasa. Last time I was here it was a 90 km journey, but as we are going over the big braided river a few kilometres from the airport the road disappears into the mountain. There's a brand-spanking-new road tunnel, just 3 km long, which replaces 50 km of driving!

Driving into Lhasa it is just one new village after another. There are huge fuel stations the size of small malls, all bright red or yellow — they must have learned from The Warehouse and their big red sheds, or perhaps it was the other way round! The main road into Lhasa proper used to be about 5 km of wide, bumpy road (about eight lanes wide, if they had had lanes marked) lined with small tenement-like stalls and shops. Now there is over 8 km of newly paved highway, just as wide as before, but lined with new-looking, cleaned-up shops. It could be that I am more used to what we would term squalor these days, but I don't think so. Crossing the main drag are partially completed flyovers, even a mini San Francisco-like spaghetti junction — very impressive.

We are back staying at the Himalaya Hotel, just as in 2004, and it isn't long before we are tucking into a beer at 'Summit Camp', the climbers' hangout just down the road from the hotel. Our every move here in Tibet is orchestrated by Dawa, who's our travel sirdar for the trip to base camp. Every expedition has to work through the Chinese and Tibetan Mountaineering Association, and all of our meals, transport and accommodation is organised by them. Like any good communist (read capitalist) business they try to maximise their returns by taking the odd short cut. Bill is constantly on the job ensuring we get what we have paid for. Some of us are pretty relaxed about it but other members of the team scream and yell over what a Kiwi would regard as minor things — like not changing money as the banks are closed, then finding the hotel rate is 7.97 yuan to the US dollar, compared to the bank's 8.0 — just get over it!

As always in Tibet, the main choice of restaurant food, and the safest, is Chinese. It's very flavoursome, and often has significant heat to it. This first night isn't too bad. I have a bit of a blocked nose, which doesn't help much, so I've woken a few times. You really can feel the thinness and the drying effect of the altitude — just think of what's to come!

2 April

Most of the team leave by bus at 9am for the Potala Palace, in what is now the centre of the new city, while Brett (the fireman from LA) and I quietly walk in the other direction. I spent a lot of time there in 2004, and being the philistine that I am I get 'templed out' pretty quickly. We walk for hours, and we do eventually get to the Potala Palace, as well as the

Jokang Temple, the old town, everywhere — always on the look-out for a café with a safe loo as we are trying to stay very hydrated! We jokingly wonder why everyone is staring at Brett; he has decided he doesn't like walking with me — apparently I attract too much attention from the locals!

I've been trying to contact Stefan Ahrens in Australia and I try yet again. Yet again I end up leaving a message on his cellphone. I had forgotten it is Sunday at home, as here everything is open, even the banks during the afternoon.

It's just another day in Lhasa really. As we walk the streets we're overwhelmed by the amount of material that's for sale and the fact that so few people are buying it. As always, through my choice to wear three-quarter pants I am the target of all sorts of responses, from stunned silence to whispers, loud exclamations, laughter and, rarely here, indifference. Continual laps through the markets finally give me a sense of direction, especially in the old city centre. It's like a maze, and not easy to find your way around due to the alleys that go in every direction. More often than not you find you arrive back at the same place. This is what Lhasa is about, though — walking steadily to keep the legs going, to acclimatise but not overdo it.

Terry, our doctor, is doing a research project on brain swelling, which is the core problem in mountain sickness. He's doing it unsupported for a personal paper, so everyone has signed up, I think. He gauges the amount of brain swelling by measuring the diameter of the optic nerve — no, he doesn't remove your eye to do it, luckily; he uses ultrasound. Why the optic nerve? Well, as I just found out, the nerve is actually an extension of the membrane that surrounds the brain, so it reflects what's happening inside the noggin. Think of holding a water balloon in your hand; the more water in the balloon the higher the pressure, and the greater the diameter of the neck of the balloon, which is just like your optic nerve. Using ultrasound Terry can see and measure the nerve. It's pretty awesome seeing your eye on screen, especially for a technophobe like me!

Unfortunately Terry lost all his kit en route to Kathmandu, though it has since been found, and will be at base camp when we arrive. He's a damn sight luckier than Todd on Cho Oyu, who didn't get his back at all.

So anyway, here's Terry arriving with just his hand luggage. Luckily that includes his ultrasound unit, but it doesn't include any of the specialised ultrasound gel. Not to be put off by this, the innovative Dr Terry finds the next best thing. We now have K-Y jelly on the end of the probe, and I can't help having second thoughts about where he is going to put it! One of my nerves was 0.4 cm, the other 0.49 cm, both indicating some brain swelling. Blood O_2 was 87, which is average, and in fact I feel better than the numbers might suggest. Often with this stuff there's a danger in knowing the numbers, because you really can't do much about it and it is easy to psyche yourself right out.

Dinner is at Snowland tonight, and in fact Brett and I had a coffee and lunch there as well. They have great food, with everything from traditional Tibetan momos and yak dishes to Chinese and western food. Even more importantly, it's safe food, so we'll do every meal there.

3 April

Heart rate 75. Not a bad night, slept well but not continuously. Cowboy didn't have the best of nights. It's temple day today — have to do it some time! The Sara Monastery on the outskirts of Lhasa turns out to be very interesting. It's much more 'real' than the Potala, though obviously not as impressive, but there are lots of normal Tibetans observing their religion. This is both humbling and somewhat puzzling. The Buddhist faith seems to support their brutally hard life, which is great for them, I guess. In fact I just wish some other religions were as supportive and benign, as faithfully observed without the fear of outside interference. In many ways the level of observance is incomprehensible to me — devotees prostrating themselves continuously for hours, days, weeks, even years on end! Their life focuses around it. Dawa, our sirdar, will do three laps of the Dojang Temple three times a week, with his wife and young daughter, and he's just a normal Tibetan. How many westerners would spend four hours plus actively practising their religion? And then not hold any other person's religion against them? It certainly works here.

The bug hit today. We all had lunch at Snowland again, as it is seen as the safest eatery here, then after lunch it was time to walk the city for a while. There was a good mountain equipment shop a few blocks away (a few bloody big blocks, but I eventually found it). In the shop I found a great down jacket — real Everest weight — but at US$350 it's too dear for me. That would suck up most of my free cash, though I am still a bit worried that my jacket is too light. It was a long walk back to the hotel, and about 3 or 4 km away the gurgling of the lower bowel became more urgent, the butt muscles tightened and the pace picked up. Only just made it into my room before lunch was lost! I was damned lucky last time to get to base camp intact. I am probably being more cautious this time, so who knows what it is. I pop a few anti-diarrhoea pills and hope for the best. If any other symptoms turn up then it will be time for some antibiotics. In the meantime I'll have a Black Russian to settle the tummy!

Dinner? Just some french fries. It's pretty hard to stuff up potatoes boiled in hot oil (I hope)!

Travellers' diarrhoea

Travellers' diarrhoea is the most common illness experienced by travellers from industrialised countries when they go to Third World countries. It is, in fact, strikingly common, with an incidence estimated from 20% to over 80%; in other words, basically everyone is going to get a dose at some time. While travellers' diarrhoea is usually a self-limiting illness, that is, you get over it eventually, it can ruin three or four days of a trip.

The primary cause of the illness is a bug. The aetiology varies with the area and the season, but the principle agents include enterotoxigenic Escherichia coli, Shigella and Salmonella species, Campylobacter jejuni, non-cholera Vibrio species, Plesiomonas shigelloides, Aeromonas species, Giardia lamblia, Entamoeba histolytica, Cryptosporidium parvum, Rotavirus and Norwalk virus.

It is common for travellers to have profound changes in their bowel habits, due to a range of factors, not least among them dietary changes. Travellers' diarrhoea is indicated by the occurrence of three or more unformed stools (runny poos!) within a 24-hour period, or any number of such unformed stools when accompanied by either nausea, vomiting, abdominal cramps or fever.

As with other enteric infections, ingestion of contaminated food and water is thought to be the most important means of contracting travellers' diarrhoea. This is why it is important to stress dietary hygiene to travellers. Although there have been many studies examining the causes of travellers' diarrhoea and its treatment, there is no consensus among the few studies that have addressed the question of whether following food and water precautions reduces the likelihood of acquiring the illness. Until further knowledge is available in this area, a common-sense approach to avoiding these enteric infections is to limit potential exposure by choosing what goes in your mouth, and washing your hands before you eat.

Avoiding the following foods, which are generally considered high-risk, helps:

- Untreated water — don't drink it, and don't brush your teeth with it!
- Ice cubes in a drink (alcohol does *not* provide protection);
- Chang (rice beer, usually made with untreated water);
- Raw vegetables and salads;
- Uncooked fish;
- Uncooked or rare-cooked meat;
- Unpeeled fruit and fresh fruit juice;
- Cheese;
- Ice cream;
- Any kind of street food, unfortunately.

In Kathmandu, some foods that have specifically been found to have a high association with subsequent diarrhoea are:

- Lassi (a yoghurt shake);
- Quiche;
- Lasagna.

Treatment issues

Although travellers' diarrhoea will usually resolve on its own, most travellers are on a limited itinerary and they don't want to spend most of it running a relay between their bed and the outhouse (if there is one). So treatment with antibiotics is often seen as a better option.

In all cases, careful attention must be paid to adequate rehydration. This is particularly important at altitude, as dehydration is a risk factor for developing altitude sickness. In cases of profound fluid loss, an electrolyte-replacement solution is preferable to plain water.

World Health Organization/UNICEF Oral Rehydration Fluid
  1 litre water (obviously, this should be disinfected,
    preferably boiled)
  10 g (2 teaspoons) sugar
  2.5 g (½ teaspoon) salt
  2.5 g (½ teaspoon) baking soda (sodium bicarbonate)

Antibiotic treatment varies depending on the cause of the diarrhoea. Unfortunately, when trekking in the mountains there is rarely a medical lab handy, and an empiric diagnosis may be the only choice.

Travellers' diarrhoea generally falls into two main groups: presumed bacterial and presumed protozoal (giardia).

Bacterial diarrhoea

Bacteria are by far the most frequent cause of travellers' diarrhoea in Nepal and Tibet, and are responsible for 70–80% of cases. Enterotoxigenic Escherichia coli is the chief cause, followed by Shigella. In general, bacterial diarrhoea is characterised by a sudden onset of 'explosive' watery diarrhoea, plus or minus any of: fever, nausea, or blood in the stool. The onset is from one to seven days after exposure, and it is usually so dramatic that patients can say exactly when they got sick.

The preferred treatment for bacterial diarrhoea in Nepal is one of the fluoroquinolone antibiotics such as norfloxacin or ciprofloxacin, but check with your doctor of course.

Protozoal diarrhoea: giardiasis

Giardia lamblia is a one-celled parasite that causes diarrhoea and gastrointestinal upset. It has a much longer incubation time than the bacterial diarrhoeas, with onset of symptoms from ten to 14 days after ingestion. The diarrhoea doesn't have the explosive onset, and is more on-again off-again in nature than bacterial diarrhoea. There may be nausea, and in some cases a fever, but the latter is less common than with bacterial diarrhoea. The preferred treatment for giardia is one of the nitroimidazole antibiotics such as tinidazole or metronidazole; again, check with your doctor. Common side effects of these medications include nausea, a bitter taste, and the possibility of a violent interaction with alcohol. *Do not drink alcohol* while on these medications, or for several days afterwards!

The great revelation of this trip has been my Derma-Seal silicone-impregnated socks, which have transformed travel and walking. I have no need of a big bag of stump socks. I have three pairs, and they will last at least three to four months. Each night I just turn them inside out and wipe them down with Savlon Gentle Wipes, and it's done — no trying to dry wet stump socks in the hotel, or worse, in the tent at below 0°C. Life is so much easier. Add to that their ability to spread the load on the stump and I can now walk like never before. I've walked kilometre after kilometre around Lhasa — no way could I have done that in 2004. You do need to wear in Derma-Seals though; it's a bit like wearing in a new pair of shoes!

I went from my well-worn socks to a new set this afternoon and am feeling very thankful that I did, as I'd forgotten how tight the new ones are. If I had changed them earlier, with all the walking of the last few days I'm sure I would have had some problems because of the tight fit.

It's time to do some miles on them, yet another few laps of Lhasa. The weather has changed to that of a winter's day, with snow and sleet coming in horizontally. The poor Tibetans at the Himalaya Hotel are stressing over my attire — shorts and my yellow shirt, as always — though in deference to the snow I have thrown on a down jacket. Well, a vest, anyway.

With the first few kilometres under the belt I'm seeing the beginning of the first pressure sores I've had with these socks. It's just a bit of skin ripped off on the tibial flare (the inside of the knee), which is easy enough to manage now, but it would be much more difficult if it happened later at base camp or advanced base camp.

Tomorrow we travel 300-plus km to Shigatse. It'll be a good rest for the stumps if I can score a good seat. (I am always early, so that shouldn't be a problem; if the worst comes to the worst I'll limp. That works every time — well, this early in the trip, anyway.) With only a few hours at the end of the day I won't be tempted to go too far. Last time this trip took nine or ten hours, I think. This time we're going by bus, which will be a bumpy trip, I bet.

After a bit more walking I popped the legs off and the right tibial flare is blistered and torn. Generally it wouldn't be too much of a problem, I would just slap a bit of 'ready set go' anti-chafe cream on and it would be healed by morning. Guess what, the cream's in my bloody base camp barrel, which is no use at all. The next best thing? Lip balm, actually. I found Chapstick worked pretty well on stump lesions on Cho Oyu when I didn't have access to my anti-chafe cream, but only time will tell tonight.

Every day is just that bit closer to base camp — closer to the focus and guts it will need to get to the top.

4 April

Heart rate at 80 this morning. That's not so crash hot when the normal resting heart rate is about 60 beats per minute. It was a pretty average night, mostly spent dreaming of the family back at home and of Anne. These big trips are in many ways so much harder; so often they are full of stories of partners moving on. We've lasted 24 years, and have a heap of years left, I think.

The high-altitude dreams are kicking in already. Here there is only 65% of the available oxygen at sea level; 50% at base camp, and only 30% on the top, if I get there! It's a wicked place to dream — must be something to do with either the lack of oxygen to the brain or else, as we now know, brain swelling.

The worst aspect of the night was the torn skin that has flared up badly on the stump, with blisters as bad as any I have seen in the 24 years of being an amputee. The tibial flare is tender, slightly swollen and very red, and the torn skin/blisters look dark and threatening. The stump is very tender to walk on and I have a slight limp, which I really hate, but at least there's a bus seat waiting!

At last we're on the road to Shigatse. Two buses, and all ready on time! Bloody amazing, both for the Tibetans and for the team! As I said, today should be nine or ten hours, at least 300 km. With mostly rough dirt roads and two passes of 5000 metres, the trip is an integral part of any journey to base camp Everest. But no, in the last eight months a new road has opened that has eliminated all the dirt road and the passes. Instead there's about 120 km of world-class road through a gorge — the trip is in essence just like a very long version of the road from Cromwell to Queenstown, the Kawarau Gorge.

What an anticlimax! I was really looking forward to the 4WD trip. Admittedly, I am a wee bit twisted. For about two-thirds of the trip I was able to do the plane-seat thing and have my legs off, resting the stumps nicely stretched out on top of the sockets. It certainly didn't do too much for my confidence seeing the angry red blotch on my right stump, especially when Bob and some of the others looked at it and went 'Oooh!' Luckily I took Bill's advice and bought a pillow and some nice hand towels in Lhasa (for base camp comfort). I spent most of the day with the stump wrapped in a clean towel and propped up on the pillow sitting on the sockets — very comfy. I just had to slip the legs on for the regular pee stop, though I must admit I was tempted to pee out the window!

After a relatively smooth four and a half hours — four and a half hours of the scale of landscape only Tibet can offer — we rolled into Shigatse, the second largest city in Tibet. We were a pretty fresh and chirpy group; well, two groups actually — the film crew were in one bus, the climbing team in the other, which was a damn good call. Lunch was at yet another great Chinese place with fantastic food — I reckon we are all putting on weight getting to base camp! Tonight we are staying at the Tibet Gang-Gyan Shigatse Hotel, on Qomolangma Road (Qomolangma is the Tibetan name for Everest), just opposite the monastery that is the home of a 26 metre high gold Buddha. It's legs off for me, though; it's time to give the wound some air. I grab some antibiotic cream off Terry, give my camera to Cowboy to shoot a few pics while he's out and about and then, as they say in business, 'put my feet up'. The breathing is pretty good here as we are only at 3900 metres; there's no noticeable difference from Lhasa really.

From previous experience (unfortunately) I know not to leave the legs off for too long or else I lose fit. That fit is always tough to get back, especially when the legs have been working so well up to now — well almost. So it's on with the Derma-Seals, the socks I have been saying heal more than damage. Well, that story has come a bit unstuck. At least I have worked out how it happened. It was my own fault entirely. As the new socks were so stiff and tight, instead of rolling them on the whole way I pulled them up the last bit, which meant that with some walking they moved, taking the skin with them.

Anyway, it's time for a walk around the block and up to the square at the monastery gates. I had forgotten how much poorer, dirtier and more inquisitive the people here are, the poorest being the Tibetans of course. It is just that much more grubby than Lhasa, though every place in Tibet and probably Nepal is pretty grubby. There are heaps of dirty kids milling around, seriously getting in my personal space, which is a concept that's foreign to them, it seems. Just a small walk down the street creates the Pied Piper syndrome, and I end up with a comet tail of kids. They're much cheekier here, getting right up behind me and imitating my walk (a piss-poor imitation, I think; I walk much better than that!). And every one of them wants to touch the legs.

Finally a bit of power-walking gets rid of them, though I am really struggling not to limp with the sore leg — can't be seen to limp, they might think I'm disabled. As the kids disappear the shop owners come out screeching for their neighbours to look — at least that's what I think they are doing — I'm not too hot on the various Chinese and Tibetan lingos. It's a bit like a Tibetan version of a Mexican wave!

More scary are the taxi drivers. As in all cities of the world one car dominates; in New York it is the Crown Victoria; in Kathmandu it's the wee Suzuki Alto (or their version anyway); in New Delhi and London the black Austin; here it is the Volkswagen Santana! You need to be bloody brave, stupid or desperate to get into one. They drive like maniacs — worse than any other driving I have seen anywhere in the world, period! Let's hope the legs hold up.

With a sore stump I am a bit like a bear with a sore head, and I can only take so much of this attention. Yes, I know, I completely brought it on myself by wearing three-quarter pants as normal. It's time to get off the street and get the legs off again. I can feel the loss of fit already, so it's lucky I got back on them. I might try to use the old sock on the right (it's thinner and will put less pressure on the wound) and see if that helps any; everything proactive is worth a try — the worst thing is to do nothing.

We eat dinner at the hotel (a pretty average Chinese meal — a bit dodgy, actually), then it's early to bed and on to New Tingri/Shegar tomorrow.

5 April

Shigatse to Shegar today. A bad night last night, with my worst sleep so far. It wasn't the breathing, but both stumps were hot and itchy. All night I could feel a rash coming on, but I couldn't see it in the torchlight. I could sure as hell feel it though! Sure enough, with daylight came tender stumps. The wound looked a wee bit better, but overall it's a worse situation to be in. Thankfully we are only travelling today.

It was an early start as well, up at 5.30am for the last good hot shower for two months or more. Breakfast was a Chinese version of a western meal — a real Chinese breakfast (i.e. dumplings, done well) would have been preferable to two slices of cold toast, dodgy jam (no butter), a bread roll, half a banana and half an apple. A few of the English film crew were less than pleased — this was not the breakfast they had signed up for!

The standard of driving yesterday was so bad we had two near-death experiences as we tried to pass trucks on blind corners, as well as other similar delights. Brett felt very, very strongly about this; as he put it, 'Talk to the bloody drivers otherwise I'll throw them off the bus and drive myself.' So Graham and Bill gave them a talking to and a more conservative approach was taken — in fact Phurba, our driver, drove at 30 kph for the first 10 km just to prove a point. It was bloody funny, and shows their typical sense of mischief.

The first 150 km were again a revelation — an all-new road through another spectacular gorge, making a short cut over two 5000 metre passes. Unfortunately it soon deteriorated into an even worse road than it had been previously, but only because they are doing a major rebuild of the whole road to Nepal — the 'Friendship Highway'. Lunch was at Lha Tse — once again Chinese, and excellent food. This isn't a climbing trip, it's a food adventure! Like Shigatse, now that we are that much further into

Tibet people seem to be even poorer and dirtier. They are definitely more intent on looking up the leg of my pants to see what else is artificial! We had some fun with the locals, then it was time to move on. I must ask Dawa if 'Tsk, tsk, tsk' means the same in Tibetan as it does in English — that's the chorus that seems to follow my travels in this country.

One feature of Lha Tse is the two rock formations that produce the huge quartz crystals that all the beggars try to sell you on the street. Another is the slate from the nearby gorge — you have never seen so much slate! Well I certainly hadn't.

There's only one pass today but it's a biggie — 5250 metres, I think. It comes on a long climb straight after Lha Tse — 1300 metres over about 20 km — and yep, it was bloody high. I felt great at the top, much better than I did in 2004, though as always at this height you need to think twice before going for a run. And run you may need to do, as within minutes of our arrival herders come begging. We strike up a deal, agreeing that if I show the ladies my legs, they'll show me theirs. There's a lot of doubt on both sides as to whether the other party has legs, and when I think about it I definitely don't want to see theirs — it would probably be the first time they had seen light in years! After we have taken a few photos and given them 1 yuan each they still cling like limpets; that is, until Cowboy gives each of them the universal currency — a can of beer. They head away happy after that.

From here it's all downhill to Shegar now. Just another typical day in Tibet, with all up just under ten hours on the bus. We are really getting high now. Shegar (which is also known as New Tingri) is at 4585 metres. We stay at the Qomolangma Hotel (yep, another hotel named Everest). The name strikes fear into trekkers and climbers worldwide, as it's renowned for its icy rooms, lack of hot water and intermittent power supply. What a bleak and desolate place this is. And there are actually people living on the street (well, one) in conditions that would kill just about anyone anywhere else — these are seriously tough people.

They're so tough, in fact, that I feel embarrassed about how I feel. I'm coping with the altitude OK, but the stump problem is huge, both mentally and physically. Mentally because I can't train; physically I'm feeling (and I am) fat, and getting fatter as we travel, eating Chinese meals two or three times a day and getting little exercise. Yes, I could eat less, but it is critical to maintain condition. It doesn't help having people like Tim, who eats like a horse (to the exclusion of other people, in fact).

One of my biggest difficulties is dealing with the whole team at mealtimes. I need to make sure I sit at another table, though it won't happen from base camp onwards. Likewise, having the film crew is a real distraction. We saw on the pass today how in-your-face they can be, and will be. Physically not doing anything is really stuffing me up. The leg is at a stage where it could end the trip if some healing doesn't start to happen. But the hardest is the head. Tomorrow I'll do a minimal walk, perhaps 100 metres, if that, as coming down will do damage — damage I can't afford. Healing here is slow, and infection very easy to get.

All in all it's a pretty shitty evening, and it's time to escape back to my room, do some writing, reading, and have what will possibly be a long night. It's time to be proactive though. In anticipation of a bad night I make a Nestlé coffee in my wee insulated Kathmandu cup, setting it up so it will all be ready in the middle of the night if I need to get up. Having a few snacks to hand also helps.

Strangely, it doesn't help that Cowboy is coping the best of anyone, I think. He's looking and feeling great — the altitude hardly seems to be having any effect on the bugger. He'll be very strong on the mountain, I think. A few of the team have blue lips already (a sign of low blood oxygen); mine have just a slight tinge, much like last time.

It's a bit of a dodgy hotel. Really, I think it is almost better to stay at somewhere like the Everest View in old Tingri, where there is nothing but food and a mattress supplied but the staff are friendly. Here they advertise everything and have nothing except the usual arrogant Chinese attitude to hotels. Never mind, it's good to have a bitch and moan to myself — base camp in one more day!

6 April

Surprisingly, I had a great sleep. There's no heating of any kind at the Qomolangma Hotel, so things are a wee bit cool. I have now been dubbed 'The Penguin'. Why? Well, at lunch today I was in my usual short-sleeved shirt while the rest of the team, and even the waiting staff, were in down!

This place is renowned for its lack of hot water — you get a big Thermos each day for drinking and washing — that's all. But there's a great little bathroom, though it's a bit dark as there is no power for most of the day (there are generators at night). So this afternoon while everyone was out I tried a wee experiment. I ran the hot tap for 15 minutes, and hey presto, hot water! I snuck in a quick shower and shave in case the amount was limited. The problem isn't that there is no hot water, but that it comes from about 400 metres away through the most poorly lagged pipes you have ever seen!

It was bloody tough today mentally as the team did an acclimatisation climb up to a monastery 300 metres above New Tingri, a fantastic-looking peak with ruins right on the summit. It was a tough day for me because if I had gone I would have done even more damage to my stumps, risking the whole trip. In the end I went in the bus with them and then went the

No insanity articles allowed

I had to copy this for you — it's typical of the type of instructions you get in Tibetan hotels. The grammar and spelling are straight from the horse's mouth.

Hotel Regulations

1. Guests are requested to show their own valid papers to prove their identities and to tell the reason for lodging when they check in at the hotel.

2. Every guest has the obligation to abide by the rules and regulations of the hotel, cooperate with the personnel in carrying out their duties and take good care of the property in the hotel.

3. No guest is allowed to up anyone for the night or let anyone use his/her own bed in the hotel.

4. We are available saft-deposit box for valuables, cash ect at front desk. Entrust local public security bureau to keep your weapon and important documents. Other wise the hotel will not be reposnsibility.

5. NO birds, domestic animals or other insanity articles are allowed to be brought into the hotel.

other way, into town, to find an internet 'café' I had heard about. After I found it I paid a few yuan for 30 minutes, then had to wait while the dude cranked up the old single-cylinder engine that drove the generator! Thank God for the internet — you can keep up with the world no matter where you are.

After that I climbed up about 50 metres above the town and whipped the leg off to give it some of the best healing possible — sun. The UV is doing heaps of good — I can see it healing in front of my eyes. It's just like at home in Hanmer Springs really, sitting up on Dunblane Peak reading a book while the dogs, Molly and Meg, run around. In this case it was minus the dogs, but with a camera in my face, as Ed turned up from nowhere and started filming. Still, it's no problem as long as they bugger off when they're told to.

6. NO inflammable, explosive, poisonous, radioactive or other dangerous articles are allowed to be carriered into the hotel. Nor is burning articles or letting off fireworks and firecrackers permitted in the hotel.

7. It is permissible to install electrical stove, microwave stove, etc. In the guest room.

8. Strictly forbid any illegal and criminal activities such as fighting, gambling, drug taking or prostitution in the hotel. No guest should put up or circulate salacious books, pictures, photos, nor play such recording or videos. And drinking excessively making great noise or playing recorder loudly in the hotel is forbidden.

9. The authority of the hotel has right to reason with anyone who has violated regulations mentioned above. Those who violate the 'Regulations Relating to the public order, Administation & punishment of the People's Republic of China' or other administrative laws will be punished by the public security organs in accordance with the law. To those who have violated the 'Criminal Laws of the People's Republic of China' the public security and judicial organs will investigate and affix their responsibilities for the crime in accordance with the law.

How about that to induce you to stay? And they mean it!

7 April

At last it's time to drive to base camp. It's another early start, so the drivers can get back to Shigatse tonight — even they don't want to stay in Shegar any longer or more often than necessary. In Shigatse they'll bolt the rear bumpers back on — they smartly removed them on the way up, obviously having learnt that they would get ripped off on this last part of the journey.

There is a pretty impressive dirt road all the way to base camp. Along the way there are three government checkpoints — more paperwork, more officious little men. The Pang La is another 5000 metre plus pass — what a road, with switchback after switchback, winding up about 1200 metres to what must be one of the best views from any road in the world. Makalu (8463 metres; the sixth highest mountain in the world), Everest and Cho Oyu are all standing proud, daring you to come closer. These are the peaks at their most impressive, looking dark, steep and forbidding — quite scary really. The 15 minutes we spend here are a time for each of us to stand alone and look out at what we have committed ourselves to. Everest just looks so much higher and harder than anything else on the planet from here.

What a road trip we had down that hill; once again, some of the most impressive winding road I have ever been on. At the bottom there are ruins and caves from about 600 years ago, which are still used for retreats by the locals even now. We are now essentially in the Rongbuk Valley, the main drainage system from the north side of Everest. We climb gradually, gaining the 1000 metres we just dropped, winding up an ever-narrowing valley, with the anticipation of the Rongbuk Monastery and the ultimate view of Everest just around the corner.

It's a pretty neat feeling rounding that corner and seeing her up close. It's not quite as scary as back on the Pang La; up here you can see the climbing lines and you get a sense of the exposure — all things we can deal with now we are just that bit closer.

The bus rolls across the plain below the terminal moraine to Russ's base camp. There's no sign of anyone except some sherpas, then Whetu appears around a tent. Then Russ. It's great to see them again. Lachhu, Phurba and the two Karsangs appear, and there's a very emotional reunion. Other sherpas appear — young Sungbow, the Tibetan kitchen boy; Tashi, a Nepalese sherpa cook; KB, a Tibetan cook; Kylar, a Nepalese sherpa cook; Chuldim, the Tibetan base camp custodian, plus a crowd of others that I will need to get to know.

Our euphoria is quickly tempered by two pieces of news. Whetu and Russ had a head-on collision on the way in, though no one was injured, luckily. Far worse news is that one of the climbing sherpas, Phurba's cousin, died two days ago from pulmonary edema — mountain sickness. He had done two quick loads up to the North Col and felt ill as he was descending. They brought him down quickly from advanced base camp on oxygen, but near base camp he collapsed. He was quickly evacuated even lower by jeep but that was to no avail, and he died on the way down. Russ is understandably very emotional; he has rarely lost anyone, and the team members are like family, so a loss really hurts. It is a salutary lesson to us all to do what we have been told, to acclimatise as instructed, and that it is an dangerous environment. You can die here, easily.

Lunch is subdued, with a memorial to Phurba's cousin, then it is time to meet up with our barrels, and all the kit that we last saw in Kathmandu. Then we have to sort out our tents, which will be home for at least the next week, and on and off for the next five weeks, maybe more.

The types of mountain sickness

High Altitude Pulmonary Edema (HAPE)
High Altitude Pulmonary Edema (or oedema) is a severe form of altitude illness, and a potentially deadly condition. It develops because the lung arteries develop excessive pressure in response to low levels of oxygen, resulting in an overflow of fluid in the lungs. Signs and symptoms of HAPE include any of the following:

- Extreme fatigue;

- Breathlessness at rest;

- Fast, shallow breathing;

- A cough, possibly productive of frothy or pink sputum;

- Gurgling or rattling breaths;

- Chest tightness, fullness, or congestion;

- Blue or grey lips or fingernails;

- Drowsiness.

HAPE usually occurs on the second night after an ascent, and is more frequent in young, fit climbers or trekkers. It may worsen with exertion.

In some people, the lack of available oxygen at high altitude causes constriction of some of the blood vessels in the lungs, shunting all of the blood through the limited number of vessels that are not constricted. This dramatically elevates the blood pressure in these vessels and results in a high-pressure leak of fluid from the blood vessels into the lungs. Exertion and cold exposure can also raise the pulmonary blood pressure and may contribute to either the onset of HAPE, or a worsening of the condition.

Immediate descent is the treatment of choice for HAPE; unless oxygen is available delay may be fatal. It is necessary to descend at least to the last elevation where the victim felt well on waking, though the descent may well be complicated by extreme fatigue, and also possibly by confusion (the result of the inability to get enough oxygen to the brain).

It is common for people with severe HAPE to develop HACE (see below), presumably due to the extremely low levels of oxygen in their blood (the equivalent of a continued rapid ascent).

HAPE usually resolves rapidly with descent, and one or two days of rest at a lower elevation may be adequate for complete recovery. Once the symptoms have fully resolved, cautious re-ascent is generally acceptable.

A summary of HAPE treatment
Descent, rest, oxygen, rehydration, and for severe cases drugs such as nifedipine, salmetreol, acetazolamide, sildenafil (or tadalafil) and dexamethasone may be used. Nifedipine, acetazolamide, sildenafil/ tadalafil and dexamethasone have all been shown to lower the pulmonary hypertensive response to hypoxia, but they are prescription medicines for a good reason — it may be hazardous to use them without appropriate medical supervision and advice. Salmetreol is more commonly used as an asthma medication, but it can also hasten the body's ability to reabsorb the edema fluid that clogs up the airways

in HAPE. It is also a prescription medication in most of the world. HAPE can be confused with a number of other respiratory conditions. For example:

- High-altitude cough and bronchitis are both characterised by a persistent cough with or without sputum production. The big difference from HAPE is that there is no shortness of breath at rest, and no severe fatigue. Normal oxygen saturations (for the altitude) can be measured if a pulse oximeter is available.

- Pneumonia can be difficult to distinguish from HAPE, though hopefully you won't end up with it at altitude — that makes life very difficult. The diagnostic test (and treatment) for this condition is descent; if it is HAPE it will improve rapidly. If the patient does not improve with descent, then there are other things going on and antibiotics need to be considered.

- Asthma might also be confused with HAPE. Fortunately, asthmatics seem to do better at altitude than at sea level — a bit like double amputees.

High Altitude Cerebral Edema (HACE)
At the 'severely ill' end of the mountain sickness spectrum is High Altitude Cerebral Edema. This is when the brain swells and ceases to function properly. HACE can progress rapidly, and can be fatal in a matter of a few hours to one or two days. People with this illness are often confused, and may not recognise that they are ill.

The hallmark of HACE is a change in mentation, or the ability to think. There may be confusion, changes in behaviour, or lethargy. There is also a characteristic loss of coordination called ataxia. This is a staggering walk that is similar to the way a person walks when they are very intoxicated on alcohol.

This loss of coordination may be subtle, and must be specifically tested for. If possible, have the sick person do a straight-line walk (the drunk-driver test). If they struggle to stay on the marked line (looking a wee bit like a high-wire balancing act), just plain can't stay on it, fall down, or can't even stand up without assistance, they fail the test and should be presumed to have HACE — or else they are seriously drunk; at altitude HACE is more likely, I think.

What to do: descend IMMEDIATELY — no choice

This is of the utmost urgency, and cannot wait (unfortunately, HACE often strikes at night). Any delay may be, and often is, fatal. The moment HACE is recognised is the moment to start organising flashlights, helpers, porters, whatever is necessary to get the person down. Other treatments include oxygen, a hyperbaric bag, and the drug dexamethasone. The latter are usually used as temporary measures until descent can be effected; they are not an alternative.

Fortunately, people with HACE usually survive if they descend soon enough and far enough.

Chapter 7

Base camp to ABC

— the real challenge

8 April

A Saturday today, I think. We change our watches back to Nepal time as soon as we arrive, as Everest is on Nepal time — tradition, I guess. I woke up twice during the night, otherwise it was a pretty good night, but crikey, the air here is a bit thin. I needed to do the coffee, bikkies and read for a while trick at 1.30am, then just read for a while at 4.30am. Before I knew it, it was almost 7am and Kylar was at the tent door with hot towels, just like on Thai Air! What an awesome way to start! It was fantastic, super-refreshing, with the temperature at -2°C. Rapidly following on his heels was Tashi with milk tea. Breakfast was toast and eggs, all sorts of mueslis and cereals, plus lots of laughing and the usual piss-taking.

It's a day of staying calm and doing as little as possible. It would be nice to have some 'Mark' time, but it is far too hot to be in the tent. They are little sun traps, and you can't leave them unzipped to get some airflow at any stage. There are two reasons for this: the first is the ultra-fine rock flour, the dust off the glacial moraine that penetrates everything; the second is the Tibetans from the shanty town, who cruise through the camp 'casing' the joint for when we head to ABC. These ratbags (who are constantly being chased out by Brett and Lachhu) are notorious for helping themselves to jackets, sleeping bags and any other thing that catches their eye. Not that you can really blame them — they live a bloody tough life and see us as extravagant people who won't miss a thing. That's OK by me on the way home, but not on the way up!

Russ has laid out a rough programme, which basically entails doing as little as possible these first few days, then gradually easing into some training on the slopes around base camp after that. We will be here for at least the next six days before deciding whether we are acclimatised enough to look at heading to interim camp next Friday, then on to ABC the day after. The bulk of the loads to kit out the expedition (high-altitude tents, sleeping bags, food and all the infrastructure of ABC) will go up tomorrow, with more yak trains going up later in the week, and us following.

In many ways I'm bloody glad there is a film crew here. It means that Max is getting them to do all his filming and not bugging us! Seriously though, I'm sure they will increasingly become a pain in the arse as the days go on — even more so as they are continually telling us they are trying not to be.

Brain swell day today! Time to have our optic nerves remeasured, though thankfully without the application of K-Y jelly this time — the real ultrasound jelly works heaps better. My brain is certainly swelling, according to Terry! But with an oxygen saturation of only 67% I don't want to know what the swelling index is — it will play with my mind too much. Additionally, if I don't know then I can't join in the typical 'pissing' contest in the mess tent of 'What's your optic nerve measurement?'

Mostly today is just a day of lazing around, though I've worked out a great system for updating the website by phone (after a bit of trial and error). The PC internet connection here isn't all that fast and Russ is having battery trouble — I sure don't want to be responsible for crashing his PCs. Anne and I tried to use her MP3 player to record the diary over the phone but it didn't pick up the weak signal well enough, then I had a brainwave (a rare occurrence, especially at altitude): use the digital answerphone. It's probably the best use it has had since I bought it for home! It worked a treat. We learn new things every day. Anne tells me I just need to talk slower now!

It's a quiet night for me, early to bed, though I think a few whisky bottles got a hammering during a game of 500 that went on late into the night (yeah, I know, many people wouldn't touch alcohol up here, but I tend to hang around with a seriously tough crowd!).

The crowded streets of old Lhasa, a continuous market.

For some reason the people of Tibet thought I was unusual —
I can't imagine why, but I got 'felt up' an awful lot.

Even in the harsh conditions at 5250 metres on the Tibetan plateau, the locals know who to ask for a beer.

Our brightly decorated mess tents were a home away from home;
needless to say, the flowers were silk and plastic.

Base Camp Everest: wake up each morning and look at the view.
No extra motivation is needed!

The puja ceremony at base camp: Russ (right) and the monks in the front row, with the team behind, on a wickedly cold and windy day. The legs were there to be blessed — every little bit helps!

9 April

Well, today I've woken up with Cowboy's head cold. A very runny nose and a worse cough than the normal hack you get at altitude (well actually, I've coughed all my life — it's how the family finds me in a crowd). The morning ritual starts off with some pill-popping: two anti-hypertension pills, one heart-safe aspirin, one anti-inflammatory (shrink that brain) and a suck on a Strepsil for the throat.

It's walk day today. Each day here seems to be defined by what you are planning on doing that's different from the day before — otherwise they all run into each other! Another brilliantly fine day, with just a light breeze. It was -5°C overnight but rapidly warms as the sun hits the tents (actually it gets too warm, hitting over 39°C in there in the early afternoon). In fact it ends up a shorts, T-shirt and jandals day, at least for the tough Kiwis.

The walk is over the terminal moraine that looms in front of base camp, probably for a couple of hours. It is very reminiscent of Cho Oyu — loose, bouldery, broken terrain, just like moraine everywhere. We check out the terminal lakes of the glacier, where our freshwater supply comes from. The boys have done an awesome job, running about 500 metres or more of alkathene pipe from the crystal-clear, ice-rimmed lakes over the moraine and down to base camp. The water runs continuously (when it isn't frozen in the pipe) into a wee pond just 'downstream' of our tents.

Whetu nearly got clobbered by a flying rock that skipped across the ice just that bit further and quicker than Woody meant it to — in fact, it missed his HD video camera by centimetres — not surprisingly, he was less than impressed. We return via the frozen stream on the true left of the glacier. In true Kiwi fashion Woody leaps over a moraine wall that's probably 30 metres tall. Cowboy follows, as you do, then some of the others also think it's a great idea — not! Even I could see the hard ice that was exposed. There was just enough moraine over it for Woody and Cowboy, but not nearly enough for anyone else. The outcome? Sore arses and various bruises! I moved to the left and pottered down some nice scree-like moraine, keeping legs and backside intact.

This evening it's beers with the film crew, checking out the kit they want us to wear (from remote mikes to harnesses with face-cams); in fact, it's mostly about bribing us — the only way they are going to entice some cooperation. As always Max and Tim are keen to have a go; I can see Max wearing a face-cam to the summit, talking the whole time. Excellent — it saves the rest of us!

10 April — Teelay's day

We have woken to our first taste of the famous base camp windstorm — huge winds blowing directly down off the slopes of Everest, buffeting everything and forcing dust into every crevice and cranny, including those on your body. It is a constant battle to keep the tent dust-free, which is especially important for my sticky Derma-Seal stump socks, which pick up every bit of floating material, and for the electronics that dominate our lives these days — cameras, PDAs, phones, chargers and MP3 players. A camera dying would be less of a tragedy than dust in the socks. Imagine wearing sandpaper for socks — that's what it would be like, I reckon.

Enough of that. Today is Teelay's day. Teelay is a double amputee I met in Tingri on the way home after the Cho Oyu climb. So much of Teelay's life mirrors mine: he lost his legs due to frostbite 20 years ago (he fell in a crevasse while crossing Nang Pa La, the 5800 metre pass, and was left for dead; it took him about six days to get out), he is about my age, and he has three children of similar ages to mine. The big difference is that Teelay has never had any legs since his double amputation in Shigatse all those years ago; in fact, for the last 20 years he has been walking around on his knees. He lost his yaks, and his livelihood, as he couldn't follow them, although he now has four yaks again as his son can work them. He retrained, learning to do leather work, and he travels around on a low pony cart.

Back in September 2004 I promised to get Teelay some legs, and to that end I had an old set of mine sent over with Russ last year. Unfortunately they weren't able to fit them on, so it's my turn to try now. Russ has sent a jeep down to Tingri to pick Teelay up, and he'll stay at base camp for as long as it takes to fit the legs.

So today Cowboy and I fitted the sockets to Teelay, and within minutes he was upright and walking inside a set of improvised parallel bars — large wooden beams we balanced on top of the blue expedition barrels — not the most stable, but with plenty of people around it seems to work. After some modifications using the materials we had brought over we were able to alter the sockets to give what I hope will be a pretty good fit. Talk about a motivated patient! He quickly understood the principles of the PTB (patella tendon bearing) socket, and what he needs to do to make them fit better. Naturally enough we had a camera in our faces all day, but that didn't deter Teelay. He is obviously a born camera-hog, and his grin is totally infectious.

To see Teelay stand and walk for the first time in 20 years was very special. I can guarantee there wasn't a dry eye in the place, though naturally everyone was blaming the wind! For me it was immensely powerful — I guess it has reiterated the power of striving to help others. What can be a small thing to us can be monumental for someone else.

What a day! This must be one of the highlights of the trip — actually, one of the highlights of my life, I reckon. Finally to be able to do something of this magnitude for a fellow human being is incredibly humbling. I must admit to feeling more than a bit shagged, though. Cowboy and I worked all day on Teelay's legs, probably not getting nearly enough rest, so by evening I was shattered. I definitely couldn't do much in the way of dinner — just a quiet dram of whisky with the usual suspects (Mark and Jen, Bob, Woody and Cowboy), then to bed was the best I could do.

11 April

I hardly slept at all last night. I was overtired, I think. If I don't get this sleeping thing sorted out then I'll need to hit Terry up for some sleeping pills, or perhaps some Benadryl to reset the pattern. The breathing's good, but I've got quite a chesty cough developing.

Bacon, eggs and beans for brekkie — awesome food in such an isolated and extreme place as this. As always, Big Tim manages to eat more than enough for three people. I'm buggered if I know how he does it. There are huge winds again today, which will make the puja ceremony less than pleasant, though it is always an emotional time.

At 9.30am, puja time, my new climbing legs are up on the chorten (a sort of altar) to be blessed. The idea is that everyone has one thing from their summit kit to be blessed during the service. The monks who have come up from the Rongbuk Monastery have so much respect and appreciation for what Russell and Terry have done for them that we get the full blessing, which is about twice as long as others I have seen, and the ceremony goes on until lunchtime. The conditions are horrendous, with a bitterly cold wind — a real gale — which is forcing smoke from the ceremonial juniper fire down our throats; even the monks have started to choke, and they just about live in smoke like that.

For many of us the puja ceremony is less about us now than about those who have gone before us. Yes, it is a blessing on our expedition, something all the sherpas and many of the climbers take very seriously. But there are few dry eyes afterwards as we think of people like Andy Harris and Rob Hall, who perished on Everest in 1996, ten years ago, and even more poignantly, Phurba's cousin who died last week helping each of us realise our dream.

At lunchtime my appetite is still not too hot, and in fact I find the amount of food Tim and Mogens can put away almost physically sickening at the moment. After picking at lunch it's back to bed. The tent is boiling hot. It's amazing really; the outside air temperature is around 5°C, while inside the thermometer in my watch, which is hanging in the centre of the tent, is reading 37°C. I read and sleep through most of the afternoon, then it is time to get up and about at 4pm. Cowboy, the bloody good man that he is, has been working with Teelay for an hour or so. He is now walking well with two sticks. Tomorrow will be time for some gait adjustment, when I can put some energy into it.

Dinnertime and still no appetite. It's worse than that, actually, as I just about chuck up a fantastic meal of lamb shanks with mash and salad. While everyone else is devouring it I am pecking away, doing 'loaded' burps. By 7.30 that's it for me, and I head to bed. As soon as I am in the cocoon that is my tent (set up with my mat, pillow, small 'table' and everything ordered) I feel heaps better. For the first time I start using my MP3 player. In fact, after a bit of Ray Charles and reading for a while, before you know it 1am has come along. How do I know that? Well, the windstorm has just bowled one of my barrels at the tent door. On go the down jacket and down booties (nothing else) and it's out the door to secure the barrel. It was bloody lucky it didn't flatten Shaun's tent next door; as it was it landed on his vestibule.

12 April

Not too bad a sleep for a change. After the barrel incident I sat up and read for an hour, had a can of beer and a nip of whisky, then slept pretty well for another four hours. Who needs sleeping tablets! There were huge winds all night. Christ, there's nothing better than an awesome storm, especially when you can hear the gusts building up from miles away, high up on the glacier, and then you just wait and wait and wait for the gust to hit — what a cool storm!

Up at 6.30am. It seems that other than the sherpas and Russ, I always seem to be the only one up early. Not that I blame the others for snuggling down in their bags, as it's as cold as a witch's tit outside. It's still blowing a gale, but as usual I find refuge in the cook tent with Russ and the sherpas.

I always treat the mornings as a bit of a challenge — the challenge is to beat the sherpas! With my Kiwi upbringing I find being delivered milk tea in bed every morning a bit hard to take. The whole servant thing isn't really where we're at — or at least it's not my thing, anyway. The more respect you have for the sherpas, the more respect they have for you, which is essential if you want to make all those little things easier — all those little things in life that become hugely important here. Like what? Like being comfortable in the cook tent grabbing some hot water or a snack, asking about washing — just about anything really. Though maybe it's just me and the way I think; in fact, I probably think too much!

It is Teelay's last day here today. Cowboy and I shorten him down some to help with his gait (I really couldn't have him taller than me) and I work on his fore–aft alignment. Within 20 minutes or less we have him walking with no poles! He is going to be one proud man when he gets home to Tingri this afternoon. I send him on his way just before lunch with a new set of legs, lots of stump socks, some of Russ's poles, a few hundred yuan in his pocket for a celebration with his family, and the potential to have a significantly better life — a very satisfying day, in fact a very satisfying week really.

His stump socks are another interesting story. Ever since I sent the legs over almost a year ago he must have been treasuring these New Zealand socks, keeping them in their own special bag, which he had made for them. It was Cowboy who pointed this out — how something we take for granted can become someone else's treasure. Crikey!

A bit of a walk is planned for this afternoon, then apparently the Discovery people want to do an interview. I'm hoping after that I'll get a snooze to recover (from the walk, not the interview). Base camp just continues on.

In the end neither the walk nor the interview happen; my throat has flared up, so no walk and definitely not enough voice for an interview — thank God!

13 April

It's definitely time for a walk today. Bill, our head guide, and Irene, our recently arrived ABC trekker, are to head to interim camp and then on to ABC on Friday. It sounds easy, but Whetu assures me it isn't. So far I have only seen about 3 km of the 22 km journey to ABC. That 3 km is only a quarter of the way to interim camp, so a bit of a challenge to come perhaps? Bill and Irene will be taking it slowly, so it sounds like my pace. Russ was pissed at the CTMA for delivering Irene 'early' by several days, as it hasn't given her enough acclimatisation time. Hence the need for a slow trip.

Now I'm up at 6.30am, beating the sherpas again — yes! I have breakfast with the sherpas this morning, in the warm confines of the cook tent. Living on the edge I even have some tsampa (roasted barley flour that you mix with sweet Sherpa tea and eat like cookie dough). Before any ride or climb I really need to get food into my gut hours before; I definitely can't do the eat-and-run thing that the rest of the guys here can do, probably because I am operating at a much higher aerobic rate than them. It is just a bloody sight harder for me, so I need to prepare that much better.

As I'm ready early (fancy that, eh?) I head off 15 minutes before the others (Bill, Irene, and a team of sherpas who are doing a carry today). It is a really enjoyable walk up the lateral moraine, with a pretty good track. On the way I meet lots of climbers and sherpas who were on Cho Oyu the same time as me. I just wander up, and after 90 minutes or so Russ, Shaun and Bob catch me up. Bill and Irene are going very slowly behind them. It is so tough on Irene as the CTMA people 'cheated' her out of two days of acclimatisation in Lhasa, the most critical time, so now she is suffering. There are no short cuts unfortunately, as she is finding out.

I am pretty slow myself, but comfortable and not pushing it. There's no need to rush just now. It's two hours to the East Rongbuk junction (most legged versions do it in 90 minutes) where the track kicks up steeply into the valley that eventually ends up at ABC, below the North Col. I am definitely not looking forward to walking back down — I'm built to go up, not down — so I head back a bit early, knowing that the others will pass me soon. I meet Bill and Irene coming up. She isn't looking too good at all, needing stops every 100 metres or so, which is not a good sign.

Going down is as bad as I thought it would be, but at least there are plenty of compulsory stops as there are about 150 yaks coming up from base camp on their way to interim and eventually ABC. The track is definitely one way, and the yaks definitely have the right of way, so it makes a great excuse for a stop. Shaun and Russ also stop every now and then to let me catch up. I will just have to get used to the embarrassment of being slow — no choice really.

14 April

A day of activity today as we all pack our ABC barrels. A large group are heading up tomorrow, with a smaller group (including Whetu, Mark and Jen, Bob and some sherpas) going on Saturday.

15 April

Time to say goodbye to the first wave of the team as they head out on the journey to ABC. It's quite exciting, but there's also a bit of fear on a few faces. From the climbing team, those who leave today include Max, Terry, Woody, Shaun, Cowboy (who sticks like glue to Woody — I hope my legs don't break!) and Big Tim. Tim thinks he might need several days to do this, so he was asked to wait and travel up the next day so he wouldn't be taking up a needed bed the next night, but as we are finding out, Big Tim likes to have things his way. From the film crew, there's Graham, Colin, Barney and Ed.

I try to update the HIMEX website but Woody has kindly nuked two PCs trying to download images to email home. Needless to say, Big Boss was less than pleased and keen to see the back of him. We, meanwhile, have been left with a somewhat touchy Big Boss! Thanks, Woody!

16 April

The first part of the big walk. The balance of our team (Bill, Mogens, Brett, Bob and me) are to head to interim camp this morning, along with Whetu, who's filming me; Jen and Doug covering the others; Simon and Jake with the big digi-Beta camera, and Dodgy following up taking still images. It's a long day, but an excellent one. It's great to be on the move again, but a pity I don't have more fitness. Luckily, a combination of good strength due to the gym work at home and the new silicone sock-liners means a relatively pain-free day. Travelling 11 km at this altitude, and also climbing over 600 metres, means there will be some very puffed and tired people crawling into interim camp tonight.

What was the 'track' like? Well, not bad until the last kilometre. Why is it always the last kilometre? Basically it's just a steadily rising, loose riverbed (moraine) that deteriorates into rock thinly covering glacier ice, steep broken sections with crevasses big enough to swallow a house (let alone me or a yak) and in places no track at all, just the outline of where the yaks have been sliding by. About halfway up, two hours before our interim camp, we stopped for a bite to eat at the site of Mallory's 1923 interim camp, which is now used by the yak 'trains' to overnight occasionally. Travelling with Bill and Whetu is fantastic. The depth of their knowledge, both from their own adventures and their historical knowledge, is enormous, and they're generally bloody funny.

It's a bit bloody cold up here, that's for sure. The pen has just given up the ghost at -10°C and it's only just after dinner (6pm). Dinner is some of Chuldim's typical fare — rice, dal bhaat and fried spam — all pretty hard to swallow after a big day and at a new altitude. Anyway, it's early to bed. Luckily I get a tent to myself — they must have heard about the snoring thing. Most importantly, that means two sleeping bags as well. Our own bags have gone on ahead on the yak train, with the rest of our ABC kit, so we're using Russ's mountain bags here. Warmth is never a problem with Russ's bags, but it is very nice to have an extra layer between you and the rocks of the moraine. There is a trick though, and that is to make sure you get the orange and black models (XL) rather than the sherpas' small

all-orange ones. And small they are — I barely fit in them, so imagine the moaning when some of the big boys got them!

I must admit the voice is a real problem. There is only just a minor squeak left really, and the throat is quite sore. It doesn't feel like much of a hole left to breathe, eat and drink. Tashi, who will be our ABC boss sherpa and cook, is having the same problem. I have been trying the traditional steam inhalation — gee, the last time I saw that was 30 or so years ago, when Dad was doing it with the same strong menthol oil as they use here. It helps a bit with the head, and certainly loosens up snot like you can't imagine, but it doesn't seem to help much with the throat.

17 April

Last chance this morning to chicken out and stay an extra day or so at interim, or do I tough it out up to ABC? As usual, my bloody-mindedness kicks in and there is no choice, so we head up the moraine for ABC. Another 11 km and 600 metres today, climbing up around the dominant Changtse corner and towards the North Col. An initial gradual climb at about a three-hour rate (according to Bill) dramatically slows in the last kilometre where we climb the last 200 metres. It seems to be the longest kilometre around. I am totally shagged, but then so it seems are most of the others.

As always, there is the bright side to everything — yes, my barrel, my kit! I have a yellow tent (HE10, to be precise) which will be my home for the rest of the expedition. I know one thing for damn sure — I am not doing that walk again until after I have climbed this hill. Not that walking up is a problem, but to walk down it would be an absolute nightmare. Never mind, I am here now. And in fact no one will be going very far for the next few days as the air here is just too thin!

Chapter 8

Life at ABC

— it's all about focus

18 April

When I wake up this morning all I can think is, 'Well, that was sure cooler than base camp.' In fact, it's much cooler even than the interim camp. Not just that, though; last night I was in for a big surprise. The sleeping bag I have up here is the smaller of my two bags, and even though it is a 'standard' in size I get claustrophobic in it. Yes, I know, pathetic. Pathetic, but possibly catastrophic, as how can I sleep without freezing? You have to want to go and climb into your 'nest' each night, and during some of the big daytime storms, and that isn't going to happen if your bag feels tighter than a coffin.

What to do? I could ask Russ for one of his expedition bags, but that's always a last resort — self-sufficiency is the name of the game here. I have worked out that if I lie on just one side, the right side, and have my down jacket on the left arm only, I can get the zip down so it feels as if there is enough room in the bag, at the same time keeping the flesh fully covered! I am very pissed off with myself, since the whole thing is the result of making a compromise back home. I was in too much of a hurry to let the Kathmandu team hunt out what I needed, which was an extra large Rumdoodle bag, and just grabbed a standard-size Moonraker — another lesson for the future!

Everyone is shagged today. Those who claim they are feeling great should look in a mirror. You need to remember that the altitude we're now at, 6400 metres, is very high. There are many people who can never make it this high, and you can only visit this altitude — you do not, cannot, live here. I'm far too tired, too puffed even to sort out my kit. I have one barrel beside my tent, but I have important kit in two other barrels that are proving very hard to find.

There is no Lachhu here to cook. When I talked to him about it he said he had done too many years at altitude; it was time for younger guys to take over while he sorts out all the expedition's problems from the comfort of base camp! Tashi, who will be our cook, has only just arrived and he is as crook as I am with a raw throat and little voice, hence the food is more Tibetan than European at the moment. This would not normally be a problem, but if you aren't the biggest fan of dal bhaat and curries every night, like me, then it's not so good. It's bloody amazing how the food we all thought was fantastic two weeks ago now seems like swill — it's still the same food; it's just the altitude that makes the difference. Everyone is moaning about it. Thank God for the barrels of snacks and the odd whisky or three.

My little yellow tent is right beside the chorten — I wonder what that means? Oh well, I'll take every bit of help I can get, because I am guaranteed to need it. We are all warned by Russ and Bill to work on our tent floors to get them smooth, as we'll be lying on that floor for at least the next three weeks or so. The sherpas were good enough to do most of the job but they still need plenty of work. Unfortunately I am too shagged to care right now; tonight I will just suffer the lumps!

19 April

Lumps? Yep, there sure were plenty of those. I would have been lucky to have got about four hours' sleep all night. Certainly there were only two times during the night when I was out cold properly. The old trick I learned from Cho Oyu — get up at midnight and have a bikkie, sweet hot coffee and read a book for an hour — doesn't seem to be as effective here. Sleep is definitely more disturbed, and the dreams are less vivid (because the sleep is not as deep).

Most importantly, though, it is 10°C colder here; between -12°C and -15°C some nights. When it is that cold several things happen. Any condensation freezes, so when you sit up and touch the tent a cascade of ice streams down the neck and into your bag; the coffee gets colder, sooner; the wee micro LED night-light that I use goes flat more quickly;

and, most importantly, any bit of you that isn't covered in layers of down or merino gets bloody cold. And my great discovery on Cho Oyu, Nestlé coffee and milk, just doesn't cut the mustard here; it doesn't taste right. The nearest thing is a mixture of PeakFuel chocolate (half a tube), a whole sachet of cappuccino powder and two teaspoons of sugar — then you are getting close. I might have to try some tea instead.

As always, there aren't many people up by the time I get up. Sometimes a sherpa, sometimes Russ, but mostly it's just Graham (one of the film producers) and me. Not that you sit around having a cup of tea for long, as it is much too cold for that, but I hate the idea of sleeping in every day. I figure it has to be better to have a wee bit of discomfort in the early hours to help you prepare for those few days up high that will be very tough. It's better to find out down here what works and what doesn't — things like how I can best get the legs on in the freezing cold of the morning.

Today I live up to my reputation as a nest-building penguin. Just like at base camp, I start to excavate an entrance for my tent. Sounds simple, doesn't it? Just a wee hole 500 mm square by 400 mm deep. At sea level in gravel it might take me five minutes perhaps? Not here. It has taken me the best part of the morning and there's still more to go.

I'm getting desperate to find my missing kit, as it has my good lithium batteries (like gold here), my spare head-lamp, another bag with leg stuff in it, and a stuff sack with some of my merino thermals — now they would be damned handy at the moment, even for the Penguin. I have just been through every suspect's barrel (with permission of course; the barrel is personal space, the place to hide your whisky!) and now it's time to move onto the expedition barrels. Unfortunately there are hundreds of these. Apparently someone saw the sherpas repacking a heap of barrels to balance out the load for the yaks. The task of searching them is a bit daunting; there are probably 60 to 80 barrels down by the 'supermarket', the large food storage tent, though with the temperatures here it's more like a walk-in freezer. There's one thing to do and that is to start.

Bugger me, only the third barrel I look in and there are my stuff sacks, along with various bits of kit that belong to others who hadn't realised it was missing! They must have too much stuff, methinks.

20 April

Another fine day — how long can this last! Each day brings bright mornings with fresh snow glistening from overnight storms and powder plumes off the ridges. That pleasant situation remains until just after the sun leaves at 3pm or so, then the cloud rolls in. Some days it comes in from over the North Col, other days it creeps up the valley from base camp. As we sit here in great weather the radio schedule reports heavy snow down at base camp, not sunshine like here — there have to be some advantages to trying to live at 6400 metres, I guess.

It's walk time again today, this time a stroll up the glacier to 'Crampon Point', the place where we leave the track worn into the rocky moraine and strike out onto the glacier itself. This is about a 15- to 20-minute jog for our sherpas. It's 45 minutes today for us mere mortals, though that doesn't include Mogens, who can run up even now. The level of fitness he has is disgusting — jeez, I wish I had some of it. It's great to see real mountaineers like Bob in their element today, striding out with a calm and steady pace that is surprisingly fast. Interestingly, I can't seem to work on the mountain like that. I find it really difficult to do that steady pace — like the sherpas I definitely prefer the dash and gasp method.

21 and 22 April

How many times can you describe a day at ABC? Life never gets much easier here. There are new challenges each day, new things to learn about your body and how it can cope with the thin soup that is the air up here. Si, our digi-Beta guy, had to be evacuated to base camp after coming down with very painful stomach cramps while in his harness filming some ice climbing. The poor bugger was in extreme pain, and then had to be taken down the mountain on the back of a Tibetan sherpa. That must have been so painful. From what we hear he walked the last ten kilometres or so; hopefully that was because his pain had diminished, rather than gotten worse on the back of a sherpa. Imagine carrying someone for 22 km; even a team of three or four taking turns. Christ, these guys are tough.

The ratbags here suggested Si just needed a decent fart! Actually, there's a bit of truth in that. A consequence of altitude that most people don't talk about is that the internal pressures need to be balanced with the lower atmospheric pressures, hence it is a fart fest! All night you can hear the symphony of the bowel, as several hundred climbers all work to balance the pressure! Anyway, Terry was worried enough to get Si down. That's the benefit of being on one of Russ's expeditions — if you need help it is there straight away.

21 April 2006 — update from Anne
Place: Home Base — New Zealand

Had a phone call from Mark last night but because of his voice he handed the phone over to Mark Whetu. Whetu said that Mark's throat is very sore and he still has no voice, and is 'very frustrated' (my words; Whetu's were somewhat stronger). From what I could understand it has been snowing for three days, with low cloud making it difficult to use the sat phones; even this call was very hard to follow, and they have no email although I think he said they were hoping to have email in about three days. They are still following their acclimatisation programme. I am clearing Mark's emails at the moment so your messages will be passed on verbally and stored in a file for him to see when he gets home; once he has email again I will send them on to him. He did send some photos but so far we have been unable to view them; we will keep working on that and hopefully get them on the website soon.

22 April 2006 — update from Anne
Place: Home Base — New Zealand

Had an email this morning from Mark saying that while he still has no voice he is feeling much better, only a slight sore throat. Says it is very high there (I assume he means in altitude). Obviously email is going, so hopefully he will do an update soon. Don't forget to keep watch on the charity meter on the Charity/Fundraising page; it is currently at $28,450. Donations can be made easily using the links on this page, and every little bit helps. Thanks, Anne

23 April

A big day today. It's time for the first climb to the North Col, the first real climbing test. I reckon the hardest part will be the first 500 metres or so up past the big Chinese camp. You are cold, it is steep, and you get an unfortunate reminder of the altitude!

Today isn't a day to rush. I have to consciously hold back otherwise I am going to end up stuffing myself trying to keep up with these 'legged' buggers. Crampon Point is a pleasant stop, though I am a bit disappointed that some of the team still haven't got things like crampon fitting sussed and need help — you shouldn't need help like that here, that's for sure.

This will be the first real test of the new climbing legs Cowboy has made for me, the C-Limbs (get it? 'Climb' = C-Limb). The rigidity of the alloy legs I had on Cho Oyu really was a boon for climbing up but it was a major pain when coming down. The C-Limbs retain the rigid fore-foot but have a flexible heel, utilising a motorcycle valve spring and the flexibility of a carbon fibre plate. In fact, the whole limb has been crafted out of carbon fibre, with a rubber Vibram sole attached to the bottom — who needs boots?

The walk across the glacier to the base of the ice wall that provides the route up to the North Col seems to go on forever. In reality it is just a kilometre or so, but it climbs up very deceptively. The start of the fixed ropes, where the slope kicks up, is where everyone seems to leave their walking poles and either just uses the fixed rope or, like me, a combination of that and an ice axe. Some people use the poles but the difficulty I had was which of my pacer poles to take — they are moulded for each hand, so do you take the left or the right? In the end, I took neither. The poles have been awesome, the envy of everyone on the hill up until now, and in fact I was dead nervous about leaving them stuck in the snow for the day in case someone decided they needed them!

What a tough climb! It's as hot as hell most of the time and when it isn't hot it's freezing cold — you can't win. Halfway up I encounter my first ladder across a crevasse, a very traditional Himalayan solution to getting over these gaping holes, which requires some significant balancing skills on my part.

Just when you think you are almost there the biggest challenge of the climb appears, a 30 metre ice cliff. Technically it's no problem as it has a rope up it, and with the sherpa traffic so far some big steps. They're a bit too big for me though — that's the problem with being a short-arse. I crawl over the lip of the cliff and what do I see? An even bigger ladder! Oh well, it can't be far now.

It's a pretty social place here on the North Col, with lots of climbers calling out 'Hi' as you go past; stopping to chat is a great excuse to take a breather. Finally, right on the lip of the col, are the two big 'homestead' tents of our expedition.

Just to be on the North Col of Everest is another lifelong dream come true. Even better, I feel damned good, though I'm not looking forward to going down. At least it is good steep ice slope, the best way to descend.

The throat has been pretty sore coming up. It feels like there is just a tiny hole to suck the air through, and that is probably right with the inflammation. I must ring Anne, but still no voice, so after dialling I pass the phone over to Woody to chat to her. At least I can let her know where I am, that I've reached another milestone on the way to the summit. I have a suck on some PeakFuel gel and slurp some drink down to rehydrate and help the throat, and then it's time for the long trip down. It's not too

April 23, 2006 — update from Anne

Place: Home Base — New Zealand

Another phone call tonight. Mark's voice slightly better but he passed the phone over to Woody to do the speaking. They walked up to the North Col today, took about four hours. This is where they phoned from. Said it was a lovely day, they would have a rest and eat some lunch before heading back to ABC, probably taking about two hours to go back down. He thought they would be at ABC for another three days recovering from today before heading up to the North Col camp for a night.

There are a couple of other sites to look at for more info from other members of the team. If you look on www.himex.com and click on NEWS you will find a couple of newsletters for the Everest Expedition. In the first newsletter there is a link to the Tigress Production blogspot; this has some diary entries from the film crew and a few photos.

painful but I seem to take at least twice as long as everyone else. That's just the way it is, I guess. In fact, the worst bit is exactly the same place as on the way up — the steep bit of moraine track between ABC and the Chinese camp. It's a bloody great relief to be back at the tent, my little yellow safety cocoon.

24 April

Just another Monday here at ABC. Time to recover from the North Col trip, not that the sherpas need to — I can hear them heading up with big loads early in the morning. The boys are playing 500 in the Big Boss's tent; from here I can hear Whetu's distinctive laugh. There will be some sore heads tomorrow, I think!

25 April

Woke up with a real start this morning. It was my first real nightmare while on the hill. Luckily I saved myself in the last second, the very second that I woke up gasping. It is one of those days really; I can't seem to walk far at all without running out of puff. Hopefully this is just another phase of acclimatisation.

The film crew and Tim are heading up to the North Col today but have got off to a pretty marginal start with all sorts of dicking around. Terry and the guides stood around looking bemused, though they eventually left us in peace. Mogens and I (with, shall we say, some firm direction from Russ) spruced up the climbing mess tent; it looked great when we had lunch in it.

Just an average Everest ABC day. Graham was running around in his 1923 Mallory clothing kit, and comparing it to Russ in his 2006 down suit and boots. His objective is to make a promo for a re-enactment of Mallory's attempt on the mountain. Good luck, because the clothing looks awfully thin, but that's just the Penguin's opinion! Then, just as the average day continues, we get an SOS. There is an Indian climber on the North Col suffering what looks like mountain sickness. He has little support, and no oxygen. Luckily for him Terry, our doc, is here, as well as our guides, Bill, Woody and Shaun, so the rescue goes full steam ahead. Oxygen is sent down from our supplies at the Col, and even as the patient is being lowered down the hill everything is under control.

Then, as always, from left field (yes, really the left field in this case, just two camps over) another call for help. A sherpa has been caught up in a gas bottle explosion and has arm injuries, apparently. They bring him over and 'Dr' Brice and Fireman Brett stabilise him. Then it's a case of waiting until Terry, the real doctor, gets down, or better still, his own team organises his evacuation — whichever happens first.

Oh that's right, things come in threes don't they? Si, our digi-Beta man, arrives back up from base camp after his evacuation a few days ago. Luckily he's made a rapid recovery. What else today? Well, I'm taking Whetu's lead and doing absolutely nothing, thanks. I have scored an extra foam mat for my tent floor (that is, I snuck down to the supply tent and liberated one from the pile), making it heaps warmer and, more importantly, safer on the stumps.

After the events of today I can't help but wonder where the 'all controlling' CTMA are. They were nowhere to be seen when the rescues needed to be done or the sherpa needed first aid — instead everyone comes to Russ. It looks very much like a 'take the money and run' scenario (about US$7000 per person for the privilege of driving across Tibet and being allowed to climb a mountain). It seems similar to some of the other environments that I have worked in, such as Fiji, Cambodia and others, where the people avoid confrontation at all costs, promise whatever you like, say yes to everything and never deliver! It wouldn't matter if they said no to stuff — as long as you know, you can plan.

So what else will this day deliver?

Not a lot for me, other than the usual poor appetite at tea time and a poorer appetite for some of the louder members of the team. I can sense a mutiny coming on; in fact, we are going to need to have a bit of team communication training, I think. It sounds like a job for Bob and me, seeing as we do it for a living. If we can't make sure this team works well we must be pretty useless! Now there is a challenge.

26 April

Russ has had a long night with the Indian. He has the sick guy in his tent, and between them he and Terry are doing hourly observations. They've got the guy on oxygen and are pumping him up with the appropriate drugs to increase his chances of survival. Russ also had to wake up even earlier than usual to arrange for the Indian's transport down to base camp (which means a 22 km trip on a sherpa's back; sounds worse than crawling). It is critical to get anyone with mountain sickness as low as possible as soon as possible to give them any chance of survival. The Indian hasn't deteriorated as expected, and in fact has shown some signs of a slight recovery. This indicates that he may have fallen victim not to mountain sickness in fact but to a stroke, which is not uncommon here unfortunately.

27 April

To the North Col again today, but this time the plan is to stay the night. I am not hugely enthusiastic about the idea. The throat is still quite sore (that 'no legs and no voice' ascent of Everest record is coming closer every day). It's been over ten days now, and while I get Terry to check that my lungs are clear every few days, the throat is very sore. The lack of voice is a real distraction too, not to mention a pain in the butt.

Everyone on the team needs to take a sleeping bag, sleeping mat and eating kit up to the North Col to help out Russ and his sherpas, though I seem to have escaped this requirement, thankfully. While it is only an extra 4 or 5 kg it seems much more in its 'psychological weight and bulk', as everyone pointedly mentions!

The walk up to Crampon Point from ABC starts steeply, up unstable moraine on a track whose surface changes every day. If plenty of sherpas and climbers have been up that's great; if more than three or four yaks have been up and down then it's not so great. Why? The hooves on each yak scatter and loosen the surface of the track and, like any bovine, they leave a continuous trail of dung. Fortunately it isn't the runny liquid jetstream of Kiwi cows; it's more solid, thanks to their marginal diet. Anyway, back to the walk. As I have said, the first part is steep and always the hardest; the legs haven't warmed up and the lungs haven't yet stretched to capacity, so you strike the toughest part in the worst condition — but then I have probably told you all this before. It is only a simple little hill but it can really mess my mind up — do ten paces, lean over panting, then look up — the top is a bloody long way! Once up to the Chinese camp the track hugs the ice wall of the glacier, still on moraine, but no yaks have been up here and the gradient is much gentler. It's a pretty serene sort of place really (I sneak away from ABC occasionally with a book and find a nice spot up here to read in peace, think, snooze, and escape).

Crampon Point is aptly named, I reckon. As I think I said earlier, the idea is to have somewhere to leave axes, crampons, etc, rather than carrying them up and down each time. The only trouble is that now we need crampons to get to Crampon Point. Granted, this was not the case earlier in the trip when the sherpas first arrived, but now it can take some tricky footwork and balance.

As always, the ascent to the North Col is a procession up the fixed ropes. I must say I felt pretty good, apart from a throat that feels like a small rusty steel tube, but frequent throat lozenges are helping a bit. I am even starting to enjoy the ladders over the crevasses, which provide a bit of variation from the continual front-pointing.

This is going to be our first night of sleeping high — well, at 7000 metres, anyway. The tents are two big family ones (we call them the 'homesteads'), each meant to sleep ten or 12. This is an innovative idea of Russ's, and an attempt to cut down on the area his expedition takes up on the North Col. The idea is to be fair to other teams, though standing here on the Col itself I can only think that every one of the other big teams has shafted him. Their sites look like a sea of yellow — there are tents for bloody miles, filling every space.

When we arrive the homesteads are revolting. The sherpas who have been using them have left them in a less than pristine condition, and I'm sure the moaning and bitching can be heard all over Everest. But before long we have them mostly straightened out — it just takes a bit of cleaning, sorting out the flooded floor, and everyone finding a space for themselves. I am lucky to have scored the smallest cubicle — a two-sherpa size, but definitely a one-Mark size by the time I spread out. Whetu is as crook as a dog; the poor bugger has picked up some sort of bug. It isn't mountain sickness, but bad stomach cramps, so we dose him up with some painkillers and hope he gets a decent sleep.

28 April

Decent sleep? I think not. Waking up in the homestead tent is about as pleasant as it was when we arrived last night — bloody awful. Like last night, good old Bob takes control of the stove and we try to get some breakfast into ourselves. Up here above ABC every individual is responsible for their own food — carrying it up, preparing it and taking any rubbish out. Cowboy and I have some shared food — a few treats like peanut butter and some nice cheese — fatty high-energy stuff that stays down.

After the less than pleasant night some of the team head down very early. Others decide on an acclimatisation climb up towards camp 2, joining the throng heading that way. Me? While heading up is an attractive idea, the concept of coming down isn't so appealing. Whetu (who has recovered from his cramps — the guy is tougher than nails), Cowboy, Woody and I decide to do some camera work further around on the Col then head down.

This is my first up-close look at the famous North Face of Everest. On the Col you are looking at it about halfway up. Under the feet it sweeps down to the glacier below in a series of snow and ice ledges, while above is the huge expanse of the upper face. Like all climbers, you look at it with one thing in mind: 'Where is the climbing line?' Actually there are numerous climbing lines, and in fact I wish that was the way we were going — now that would be cool. The one thing I will be doing in a few weeks' time is traversing the very top of this face; below the feet will be a drop of 3000 metres, enough to create the odd nervous butterfly, I can tell you!

As I hate people having to wait for me I send the others ahead. Whetu will come down later. It's no problem arm rapping down the fixed lines; if you can't be trusted to do that by yourself then I figure you aren't a mountaineer's bum really — unfortunately that description fits quite a few on this hill. Enviously I watch Cowboy and some of the others glide down, while my descent is best described as a stagger and stumble. We still haven't cracked this downhill thing. The climbing legs are far too active for my short stumps, so by the time I am halfway down things are getting painful. This means there's no elegance in the movement — in fact I run the risk of looking like a double amputee — damn!

I'm feeling pretty proud of myself for mastering the exposed small ice-cliff, and two-thirds of the way I lean onto the rope to continue the arm rap. Instantly the world turns upside down — turns from a cruisy descent into a flurry of snow and confusion. After what feels like two somersaults instinct takes over and I self-arrest in the best traditions of mountaineering, sliding to a stop just above where the slope flattens out a bit. Time for a body check. Spit the snow out of the mouth, shake it out of the hair, trying not to dump it all down my neck, drop the pack and get up to look around — what the hell happened? Instantly I topple, worse than if I was drunk! I look down, and 'Oops — Cowboy isn't going to like this.' The foot has come right off the pylon. If it had not been for the duct tape holding the excess crampon strap out of the way up on the pylon I would have lost the foot completely. I can just see it in my mind's eye toppling down a crevasse, gone for good.

It's time to take stock. Firstly, it's no use being on the rope as the anchor above me has pulled out — the snow stake has popped right out. There are heaps of people coming up the slope below, out of sight, and they are all pulling hard on the rope, pulling me over, so I unclip fast. I croak out a warning to them not to pull but no one listens. Two sherpas go by and don't even stop. Not that I mind, but they don't even fix the anchor. I haul the radio out of the pack and call ABC.

'Russ, I have a wee issue, mate. I've broken my leg.'

Imagine the consternation among the other teams listening in on our frequency when he replies that I'm a useless prick, he can't take me anywhere, and why don't I just bolt on a new one? I ask if one of the sherpas can bring up the spare climbing leg, and tell him I'll have a go at trying to fix the broken one, once I have sussed out if it is possible. Cowboy then comes on the radio to say he will bring up one of my walking legs from Crampon Point, as he has just arrived there — well, that seems like justice, since he made the leg!

Suddenly Whetu comes hurtling around the corner of the ice-cliff and down to me, camera in hand of course. How the hell did he get here so fast — only minutes ago he was with the sherpas on the North Col hundreds of metres above. Christ, it has taken me a good 25 to 30 minutes to descend this far; he must have done it in five minutes! Someone on the radio asks Whetu to help me, to which he replies that, one, he is the camera and is recording events — he's not a guide; and two, the Penguin is perfectly capable of helping himself! Dead right on both counts.

I'm now about 100 vertical metres above the glacier — and they are just about vertical — and looking down I can see the ant-like figures of Cowboy and Bob, I think, scurrying (well, more like crawling) towards the base of the climb. It's time to be a bit proactive. It looks as if the shaft of the leg (my 'shin') has popped out of the foot-piece. I would say that landing down hard like that has meant the rubber bumper stop has over-compressed, and so has the motorcycle valve spring under the shaft, breaking the resin bond and forcing the shaft up and out. Therefore all I should need to do is force it back into its hole, tape the whole thing up with duct tape and walk very carefully — easy peasy, as they say.

With a bit of stomping (well, it's already broken, so it won't matter if I shag it a wee bit more) the shaft goes in most of the way. Luckily I always carry heaps of duct tape. After a tentative step or two I reckon I can get myself down, especially when there is a fixed rope the whole way. There'll be no arm rapping this time — just careful, considered step after step.

A very puffed Cowboy appears with the walking leg but my repair is still working so we push on. Bob, being the experienced climber that he is, positions himself just below me to shorten the distance of the fall they all think will happen. I'm a bit of a stubborn bugger, though, and have absolutely no intention of falling. Thankfully the duct tape holds all the way down to the base, where I swap to the walking leg and have a go at fitting the crampon to it. It's not overly successful, but I'll give it a whirl anyway. Well, it lasted 100 metres before flipping off — not that I really need it. I've seen sherpas up here in just their old-style sandshoes, or is that new style these days — light canvas uppers and a crepe-like rubber sole. My ultra-light climbing boot will be just fine.

I now have an insight into what it must be like for a single amputee. On the right leg I have my 'flex foot' and on the left my C-Limb, Cowboy's climbing leg. The result is a lopsided gait down the glacier, the odd bit of slipping and sliding, but also a wee bit of a revelation. The flex-foot works better here in the flatter country than the C-Limb, especially when the slope is just slight to moderate downhill. The C-Limb is still too active for my short stumps and less-than-perfect quad muscles, throwing me over the knee as the spring in the foot activates when the foot flattens on the ground. I now know why this last bit always seems so tough; I have already done the damage to the stump and muscles before I get there. Live and learn from everything.

29 April

Well, I have found out why we go high to acclimatise then back down. I have just woken from my best night's sleep ever. It's a quiet day today, one on which to rest and relax even if you don't want to, and to recover from yesterday's excitement. Cowboy also needs to fix the leg. We have a spare, but it will be better to fix this one and keep the spare as just that — spare. There doesn't seem to be a lot of action, though. It must all be happening in his head — you know what these inventor types are like!

30 April

Another great night's sleep. No bad dreams, or dreams of any sort really. The best Sunday lie-in my life, I think, especially after the last few weeks. At 5.30 I can hear the sherpas preparing for a load carry to the North Col, and then for some to stay as support for the big event of the day — Phurba and five others are heading to the summit today from 7900 metres (camp 3), fixing rope from their high point of 8300 metres, I think, just below camp 4.

All the radios are on this morning. Russ gives the camera guy at the North Col a rev up when he reckons it is too windy and cold to film, just after sun up. After some strong directives from Russ they are hopefully set up in one of the wee tents out on the edge of the col with a view of the summit. From there they can film the boys on the summit push, as well as being ready to film the sherpas from ABC dropping their loads of oxygen then heading down. Big Tim sounds fine on the radio from the North Col. He seems to be doing everything several days behind us, as there is always a drama of some sort looming. When I say he sounds fine, I mean not necessarily pleased, but fine; it has been a big effort for him to catch up after a lot of setbacks. I hope his trip downhill will be relatively pain- and event-free, though I have a sneaking suspicion there will be some story to top mine!

Critical, cynical me. I need to slap my hand as Tim arrives back just as over the top as always; every minute is definitely a loud adventure with him around.

It's time to push Cowboy on the leg repairs today. Getting him started is always a little tough, but started we are. As the afternoon clicks over we are anxiously watching for the summit team, listening in on the radio minute by minute. I'm pretty shagged, so I spend the afternoon lying in the tent, having the odd snooze with the radio on following Phurba's progress. At 15.05 hours on 30 April, we have the earliest summit of Everest ever in a season, we think! Impressively, it's a summit push that has been totally built by those six guys over the last five weeks — they put in all the camps and set up the fixed rope for us, and summited as well! Their next job is to get off safely, and get home.

While we all think they will try for the 7500 metre camp 2 or North Col, they have different ideas. Around five hours and 50 minutes later, at about 8.45pm, I think, they walk into ABC, down from the summit of Everest. These guys are awesome. They are still walking well, chatting and humble. What an achievement, and they are just worried that each other is OK and that Tashi has tea on for them.

Never having been one for getting into the mob excitement, I wait by my tent at the entrance to our 'main street' with my head-lamp shining the way. Every one of them says thanks to me, gives me a polite shake of the hand — hell, they didn't need to do anything! Phurba brought tears to my eyes when after a 19-hour day he stopped for a hug and asked after my throat and voice; 'It needs to be fixed so we can go back together soon' was his comment!

On that note it was bed for me. Russ had warned us earlier in the night to be ready to do things a wee bit differently from the previous year's programme, as it was so early in the season. Hence I didn't have the most stable sleep that night, the result of excitement rather than nervousness! A good thing.

The summit team, 30 April 2006

Phurba Tashi, Nepalese, ten times summit
Son Dorjee, Nepalese, three times summit
Dorji Somam Gyalson, Nepalese, five times summit
Ta Shi Ping Tso, Tibetan, four times summit
Denzeong, Tibetan, three times summit
Ta Shi Tsenzong, Tibetan, two times summit

1 May

I am woken by the 'orcs', as we call them — the early-morning procession of sherpas heading to the North Col with their loads. They're a mixture of our sherpas and those from other expeditions, all coughing in the cold air at 5am, snorting, snotting, grunting and farting. That's just for a start — then there is the crunch of rocks and gravel, the creak of frozen snow — I'm quite sure they must have been extras in *The Lord of the Rings*.

Meanwhile, it's time to pinch our collective selves. Six sherpas on the summit yesterday. And just to make things more difficult for themselves they went from ABC to the summit and back to ABC in three days while fixing the last 600 metres of rope on the roof of the world. Actually it was probably nearer 700 metres, as they kicked the last bit down the south side. Now that was cheeky!

It's a tough wake-up procedure, as it has been for a while now. Imagine this — as I move from horizontal to sitting up, the bucket of snot that is my sinus cavities these days (actually the whole skull, if the truth were known) sloshes backwards and forwards, trying to slop over into my lungs, creating a lovely choking feeling. After the obligatory three or four minutes of trying to vomit or sneeze, the snot comes out — 90% out the nose, the other 10% out as a big bloody coughed-up goober.

This has been the morning ritual for almost ten days now. In fact, it isn't just the morning ritual, it happens any time when I'm pushing the body really hard, the air is really cold or it's just too bloody high — bend over, cough, snort, choke, try to vomit, general puke time. It leaves you gasping like a fish out of water, and it's quite scary, whether it's in daylight halfway up the ropes or in the middle of the night when you wake up for a pee. The question I ask each day is what to do about it?

I'm trying to have two or three vapour steams each day, which helps a bit. Drugs? That would be a nice easy solution, but it never works out like that. Anti-inflammatory pills seem to be the advice of Dr Terry, though I am very tempted to do some antibiotics, anything to shake loose that bucket of snot.

As a kid my lungs were always full of snot — just ask my mum. We used all sorts of drugs and physical therapies to loosen it, including the good old 'lay on your tummy on the bed with your chin over the edge and cough while Mum bangs away on your back' trick. I think they call it massage these days. But hell, it worked — I coughed up some great goobers. That, thankfully, isn't the problem so much here. The lungs are clear, and I intend to keep them that way! The biggest issue is the choking. Time to work on it, I reckon.

I definitely need to stretch the legs today, so after a few chores it's time to pack up and do what I call my Hanmer Springs thing — book, food and sunshine — you can't beat it. I pack the backpack with the latest novel I am struggling through, a drink (though I am choking at the thought already), duvet jacket just in case the weather does its usual trick and craps out, lunch, and lastly a radio so if I get lost or do a leg thing I can get help.

After 10 metres I'm stuffed. This can't be right — I'm acclimatised, right? But yep, it still hurts. I plod on towards Crampon Point; hyper-ventilating helps, I think, though it doesn't sound or look particularly professional. Near Crampon Point I hang a left, out onto the unstable rock ridge that is the lateral moraine of the glacier. I find a nice little possie that is out of the wind; while the sun is shining, the wind will lower the apparent temperature to near 0°.

Ensconced behind my newly created wee rock wall (thanks to my jobs on farms when I was a kid, I'm a dab hand at dry stone walling) the clothes start to come off. Don't worry, not enough to scare the natives, but enough to get some sun on the body. After an hour I have just about fried my arse! Lying there reading in the sun with my picnic lunch, looking straight up at 8850 metres, the summit of the world, I think, who needs to climb it? I could lie there all day, all my life. But after three hours it's time to get back to real life. As I stand up to pack my things I see that I have made my possie right on the edge of a deep disguised crevasse — another hour in the sun and my little sun-worshipper's capsule would have slid straight in. Now that would have been difficult to explain to Russ when he had to come and pull me out.

I race the advancing afternoon snowstorm back to camp, 'race' being very much a relative term for me at this altitude. Shock, horror, intense disappointment — I've missed a piss-up! Everyone is just finishing up Sprites, Cokes, beers and whiskies while celebrating the boys' achievement yesterday. Not only that, but Russ has apparently laid out the plan for the next two weeks. Everyone is totally hyped and I'm standing around looking like the village idiot — no problem there, it's very much in style! No really, I didn't feel left out at all. I knew Russ would keep me in the loop, in the same way as I knew exactly what his plan was.

I think that of anyone on this wee adventure I am lucky enough both to understand what's happening (I know the people so well, and know climbing from a lifetime of experience) and to have complete faith in the leadership — and not just in their decisions, but in their ability to argue the point with me when required.

As I arrive the snow does too and the party splits up. Never mind, I'm sure I can scrounge a whisky somewhere. Before I turned up with the snow Russ had given the team what I would call an attitude adjustment. He filled a pack with what each of the boys took up to the summit — oxygen bottles, rope for the fixed lines, drinks, food — all up about 30 kg! A superhuman effort!

Today is one of the last chances to send a video message home. Whetu has set up the camera for me, and I try to have a chat to Anne and the family, but it isn't going at all well. Quite apart from my voice breaking up, just the thought of the family so far away, combined with the enormity of the task I have set myself, means the message is pretty emotional and less than positive. Oh well, I guess it shows just how damned tough it is for me at the moment.

I am sitting here tonight at 5.30 in the radio alcove of Russ's homestead tent, which is the best place to write in camp. Phurba, Dawa, Russ and Barney are doing a radio schedule, and Phurba is talking to Lachhu. The resulting noise sounds like music, very similar to the Brian Ferry playing in the background — sounds of home! It's really comforting sitting here, it's so much like family. Earlier the film crew were having one of their usual discussions; it's amazing to hear so much bureaucratic crap at 6400 metres! While he's on the radio Barney makes some comment on the weather forecast — actually, it's 'our' weather forecast — and gets jumped on by us all. It's easy to forget that it is very much our info, and you can guarantee every other team on this mountain is listening in for snippets like that! We all have a bit of learning to do yet — not so much about climbing; more about the politics of being here. Most importantly though, I hope Lachhu has found my whisky!

The odd beer, wine and whisky made their appearance in the dining tent. There are going to be some people with sore heads tomorrow — you are a very cheap drunk at ABC!

2 May

This is another morning where the early light has the effect of electrifying the tent at 5.30am after a night of snow and huge winds. The winds are still buffeting the tent, so it's time to snuggle down and consider the usual morning options:

1. Stay right here until late am — called doing a Cowboy;

2. Accept a towel then milk tea from the sherpas at 7am;

3. Beat them at their own game.

Yep, that's the go. The dressing technique in these temperatures is based around slowly dressing various bits of the body while still inside the sleeping bag, until you are finally ready to pop out. I unzip the tent at 6.15 to reveal brilliant sunshine, so I sit there in my 'lounge lizard' chair warming up, checking out who is up (as usual, just Russ, Bill and some sherpas) while putting the legs on. Once upright it is straight to that haven, the cook tent, unless of course the bladder demands attention en route. Then it's time to stoke the metabolic fires with the first coffee for the day. The cook tent coffee is always the best, as it's made with Big Boss Russ in mind.

What an exciting time of the day. Russ, Bill, Phurba, Terry, all the usual suspects, are planning the day, chatting and bonding — it's definitely the place to be. This morning, though, Russ has a confession. A yak boy arrived at his tent yesterday with a bottle of Glenfiddich from base camp, 'for Mark', so naturally Russ passed it on to Mark 1, bloody Whetu! Now we all know what that means. Yep, the film crew scoffed my whisky! There's not even a drop left in the bottle when I go to collect the evidence. Never mind, in atonement I get directions to the holy grail, barrel number . . . the good whisky barrel. (Of course I am not so dumb as to let you all know the number!)

In all it's a productive morning. It's just a pity the rest of the day isn't quite so productive. While Russ, Ed and Woody head down to base camp to collect and check out much of the camera stuff for the summit push,

I take advantage of the fine weather to do a supplementary to yesterday's video message home. Try talking into a Beta camera while it's snowing, you have no voice, and have the big hammer of emotion hitting you hard — it's lucky I was wearing my sunglasses. It's a terrible thing I am about to put my family through, but it is real, it is real. I'm not so sure that part two of the video will help much, but at least this morning I have a voice, that's something.

Today I had the world's worst 'fur ball'; a coughing and choking/upchucking fit, with several small pukes just to top it off. I even got several people out of their tents, which was bloody impressive. That was the day really, with a bit of a snooze. That's ABC.

Tonight the sherpas are winding up for a biggie. They have a day off tomorrow, and have access to the odd brandy (the number one tipple for those of them who drink) so the singing is already loud, and the stamp of the dance is making the whole glacier vibrate. I can't face dinner tonight — just another dram of whisky and then to bed. The bloody throat — you can feel it swelling like a dam with chunky snot behind it. It would be better if it burst!

3 May

This is perhaps not just another ABC day, as things are getting more complicated the longer we stay here, especially with the complex mixture of personalities that have been assembled. It's about now that the really tough time comes along, with bored, stressed people who forget that they are living in comparative luxury at 6400 metres. If only I had a voice, I'd remind the odd person here how bloody lucky they are — try being here with no voice, no communication with your family, no easy intervention in discussions. Bugger being cold, putting up with a lumpy bed, food you don't necessarily like, shitting in a bucket, feeling like you are hung over — that's nothing to the tough things in life. Those gold standards that some of us have been shown mean that this is really a bit of a holiday camp. Treat it like one, and all of a sudden everything becomes just that much easier. It's still not pleasant, but the idea is to put up with it. Sorry to harp on in this vein, but as I said, it's that time of the trip. I could easily go into personalities, but should I?

Yeah why not, it's that time of the trip!

Brett — the LA fireman, at the moment a bit stressed and panicking, on sleeping pills and plenty of other medications to help with the tough environment. He is a wee bit quick to rise to a situation in the mess tent but a very caring guy. A macho man but even down here he is looking crook all the time, which is possibly reflected in a sharp negative barb when you least expect it. It is a tough place here.

Tim — this guy is a champion. I've never heard anyone, anywhere, vocalise their every feeling, breath and bodily function the way he does. It's like 110 kg of Tourette's syndrome, but in reality it's just a 110 kg combination of what a Kiwi would see as bad manners and a touch of attention-seeking (but then we are critical bastards!). He eats like a horse even up here — in fact, he makes this part of his brand — but for a biker, in fact like most bikers I know, and I know a few, he's soft. As soon as the going gets tough — that's mountaineering tough — he finds an excuse to do something else, which I totally understand, as I try unsuccessfully to do it myself!

Max — the Energizer bunny with the diversionary chip. Full of questions (great) but unfortunately just asked the same ones for the fifth time (not great). Expeditions are his life — to be the first Lebanese to do lots of stuff — but I must admit that hell, if I did adventures the way he does (and I have done occasionally) I would be roasted by the media (and have been; remember Mount Cook?). He's like your overactive nephew — his dream, his needs, frequently rollercoaster over the top of others — but he has a heart of gold. Actually, everyone does up here.

Bob — early 50s, like me a motivator, but unlike me very 'Zen'. Calls a spade a spade; actually, being an Aussie, he calls it a fucking spade. He's starting to stress now he has the sore throat, but there's only minor blame directed my way. He has been to 8500 metres before (in 2001, with Whetu) and like me has climbed many peaks. In fact, like me he's one of the only 'real climbers' on the team, but unfortunately that idea sometimes stresses him out a wee bit! He has the ability to be a strong mediator and frequently is, but then occasionally he is very critical of the need for it. He's extremely caring to me; some of the others see him in a less positive light at times though.

These are the guys I meet, talk with and interact with every day. This is what expeditions are about; sure there are others, but it is the inner circle that impacts so hugely on your thinking, your mind, your attitude.

4 May

The North Col again today. A great chance to try out the leg repairs, and the last real test of the body before the proposed summit push in four days or so. Apart from having to stop halfway up to clear the snot fur ball and just about puke my guts out, it has been an awesome day. I found a solution to the worst of the throat — chewing gum! Brett's sister has sent him a pretty awesome 'Red Cross' parcel that is full of food

4 May 2006 — update from Anne
Place: Home Base — New Zealand

Just had a phone message from Mark to say he is about to go up to the North Col for a couple of nights and then return to ABC (advanced base camp). His voice was a lot better although he thought he would lose it again once he got up higher. At the moment they are looking at summiting some time towards the end of May, but he is unable to give definite dates.

8 May 2006 — update from Anne
Place: Home Base — New Zealand

Mark hasn't been able to get to the computer much lately. He has rung quite a few times over the past few days now he is getting his voice back. When he rang on Saturday he was sitting in his tent doorway sunbathing, but the next time we talked to him a few hours later it was snowing again. Hard to imagine, isn't it.

He has been up to the North Col again for one night and then came back to ABC, where he will now stay and wait until the time is right to attempt the summit. A very boring process, and frustrating, I imagine.

Playing on the ice-cliffs beside ABC to test the legs.

At home in my little tent at ABC, beside the chorten; behind are the ice-cliffs leading up to the North Col.

Shaun climbing above camp 3, breathing the vital oxygen and following the fixed rope.

2006 versus 1923: Russ (left) in a modern down suit, while Graham models a replica of Mallory's wool and silk clothing; I know which I prefer!

Oops — the busted C-Limb on the descent from the North Col;
it's lucky I am an amputee and can just bolt on a new one!

10 May and the summit push begins — the ant trail of climbers heading up to the North Col.

4pm, 14 May, the upper slopes of Everest. Look closely and you will see people at the first and second steps — just one more day to go.

Typical terrain on the north side of Everest: bluffs, ledges, and always the summit in sight above.

treats, including several packs of gum. With some negotiation (I think it is called begging) I score a pack; it's like gold here.

On the col today we stored some food ready for the summit days, as the less we have to carry next time the better. A few of our sherpas are passing through after carrying loads up high, so we fill them up on Sherpa tea. One of the boys has a throat as bad as mine, so a piece of gum heads his way — I know how he feels.

9 May

Well, we are ready. Today team 1 headed out of ABC for the North Col and higher, planning at this stage to summit on Saturday 13 May. Team 2 will follow tomorrow, with summit day planned for Sunday 14 May.

This is an exciting time for everyone but a nerve-racking time for Russ. He is stage-managing the whole show, especially using his expertise to schedule summit weather for us. We have chosen to head for the summit instead of having the traditional rest at base camp because all the team is in great health and the calm weather has not worn them out. To trudge the 22 km down to BC then back to ABC just does not seem to add enough value to our summit aspirations.

Why divide into two teams? There are several reasons for this, but it's mostly to limit congestion on summit day and maximise logistics.

Speaking of logistics, this year Russ has had his sherpas fix all the rope on the north of Everest (from the bottom of the North Col wall to the very summit) to ensure the safety of all climbers. This has come at a cost, as it includes 5400 metres of rope, freight, taxes, anchor gear, sherpas' wages and their safety gear (including oxygen). The total cost is over US$32,000! The ropes look like a highway. The only problem is recovering the cost, as all the climbers are using the ropes. The extra cost is only US$100 per climber (sherpas are free), but so far only 12 expeditions have paid up (a total of US$11,600) and HIMEX is currently shouldering the extra cost.

The conditions and weather have so far been excellent this year; we are hoping it continues that way, giving us the opportunity to fulfil our dreams. At least the clients feel in safe hands — between the guides, sherpas and film crew there are 63 ascents of Everest. This is a huge amount of experience, and the clients are keen to add to the number of ascents.

So who is in teams 1 and 2?

Team 1

Bill (head guide, four summits) and Phinjo (Tibetan)

Ken (camera, one summit) and Narwang (Tibetan, two summits)

Terry ('Doc') and Karsang Namgel (Nepalese, five summits)

Marcel (client) and Loppsang Temba (Nepalese, five summits)

Kurt (client) and Pema Chhosang (Nepalese)

Brett (client) and Phura Nuru (Nepalese)

Mogens (super-fit client, no oxygen!) and Tashi Teshering (Tibetan, two summits)

Ed (camera) and Ngawang Nurbu (Nepalese)

Team 2

Woody (guide, two summits) and Phurba Tashi (Nepalese, ten summits — that is a lot of summits!)

Shaun (guide) and Wangbe (Tibetan)

Whetu (camera, three summits) and Son Dorgee (Nepalese, four summits)

Cowboy (client) and Tashi Phinjo (Tibetan, three summits)

Penguin (client no-legs) and Dorji Sonam Gyalgen (Nepalese, five summits)

Bob (client) and Phubu Tsering (Tibetan, two summits)

Gerard (client, 62 years old) and Tenzing (Tibetan, three summits)

Max (client) and Dorjee (Tibetan)

Tim (client) and Lhakpa Nuru (Nepalese)

Jen (camera) and Tashi Namgye (Tibetan)

North Col logistics and film crew

Russ (team leader, four summits)

Doug (film crew and master wildlife photographer, 'Mr Polar Bear')

Jake (soundy and ex-rock star)

Luo Bu Zhan Duz (supporting sherpa for North Col, Tibetan)

The summit of Everest

— the summit of achievement

10 May

It's the anniversary of Rob Hall and Andy Harris's death on this hill, ten years ago today. It was such a tragic day for so many. On the one hand it seems as though it happened just yesterday, while on the other it's as if it was in another life. Either way, it brought a tear to my eye as I lit two sticks of incense on the chorten to pay my respects. Those of us who knew the guys were quiet when it was time to head up the hill, time for the summit bid. It was strange, really; it should be a time of celebration, rather than one of nerves.

Anne's 'virtual letter' on a CD has arrived. The boys brought it up from base camp last night but there wasn't a PC going, or able to go (too cold, and flat batteries) so this morning is my only chance to 'see' Anne. But again I need a PC to watch it on, and of course Barney and Co want to film it.

I live my life being early, but that wasn't going to happen today, of all days. When the film crew is involved (any film crew, anywhere, no matter what they say), time stretches. I want to be off by about 9.30 but I think that means 11.30 in film time. Unfortunately the combination of a cold PC (as always in the morning), a 'hot' and stressed Russ, several people's emails to be cleared before the summit push, as well as the latest weather downloads, all conspires to delay the viewing, hence my departure. The film crew know I want to get away and so cause even more stress by trying to push Russ. The only problem is that you can't push Russ; in this case it's an abrupt, 'Fuck off; everything else is more important.'

While trying to remain cool on the outside I am stressing hugely inside. This day of all days needs to go right or the whole tone of the trip will be fucked up. I desperately hate being away 'late', but I guess it is a case of never mind, time to practise chilling out. Being late away won't really matter, but it is the principle that the filming is more important than my climb that pisses me off. If it wasn't Anne on that CD I'd be out of here. Add to that the fact that someone's emails, which they can download any time, are more important than my climb, and that's the stuff that stresses.

Finally I get to see one minute 46 seconds of Anne. It's great to see her, but a pity it has to be in this format, rather than just chatting away on the phone. Then there are the usual dumb on-camera questions, which I manage to answer in my croaky voice, and it is time to say a few goodbyes. Well, more 'See you in a few days.' Then at last I'm heading up the steep moraine slope past the Chinese camp. It's disturbingly painful. Christ, what's it going to be like higher up?

I feel almost like a fraud as people call out 'Summit?' and I croak back or just nod. It is so hard to gauge whether their responses are patronising or genuinely supportive; at least the Tibetans are refreshingly upfront, mostly still gobsmacked that I'd be dumb enough to even be here.

Pace yourself, Mark, stay away from everyone. Whetu wants to film the walk up the moraine, which gives me an excuse to take a rest on a boulder while I wait for him to rush on ahead to film, or wait for him to catch up after I've walked past. Who would want to be a cameraman on Everest? Bugger that! To do a good job — and Whetu does an awesome job — he has to be stronger, fitter and a more talented climber than anyone else, and he gets to go twice as far, twice as fast!

There is a feeling of excitement as I swap legs at Crampon Point. This is it — the last trip up the ice-cliffs to the North Col. Up higher on the mountain our number one team are just a day ahead, moving up the ice slope towards camp 2. From now on everything has to work like clockwork. They need to clear the camp before we arrive as there just isn't room for the whole team in the higher camps. The North Col ropes are crowded, with traffic going both ways, though there are more going up at the moment than coming down. This is a bit of a worry, as it means a crowded mountain up high. Naively, we had thought we might be able to sneak away and have the mountain to ourselves!

It's a pretty uneventful trip up. The throat is feeling like the usual rusty hole, but that's about all. News that I'm on my way to the summit has travelled up the hill, and as I move through the tents below the last ladder over the big crevasse, just below our homestead tents, lots of climbers and sherpas come out to say good luck. It's all pretty humbling, that's for sure.

There's a big surprise at camp 1 on the Col. Brett is here and not looking well. Apparently he had made it a few hundred metres above the Col that morning before pulling the pin on the whole idea. He was feeling sick — real vomiting sick — with head spins and the like, and he makes it abundantly clear that he has made his decision. Everyone is trying to convince him to have another go, but hell, after two trips to Everest if he doesn't want it or can't do it then leave the poor bugger alone. He has got higher on the hill this year than last, I think.

It is really important that I don't let his feelings and situation impinge on my thinking, drive and desire. I offer him some words, but Everest isn't the place to push people. Push yourself, most definitely, as you won't make it otherwise, but never push other people on the way up.

Brett packs up his stuff and radios down to ask for help to carry his kit down, but Russ has all the sherpas committed to the teams going up. Brett will have several days in which to do a few trips with his gear, and that's what it will take — jeez, he has some kit!

The homestead tents are a bit better set up than before and we can spread out heaps more this time. (Heaps more? Well, everything is relative, isn't it, especially here.) I manage to score my little cubbyhole again. Woody is playing mother with the Primus stove this time, hot fluids being the basis of our life up here. A few crackers with some cheese and crunchy peanut butter set new standards in mountain cuisine.

The weather isn't quite the perfect days we have experienced up till now. There's some wind up high, and the potential for more over the next few days, which to put it bluntly scares me shitless. The wind was our undoing in 1982. I know what it is like to be out in that sort of storm, and even light winds up here will be bloody tough. Add to that the instability of being a double amputee; the envelope I can operate in is much smaller than legged versions, and the wind forecast — rising from 20 kph to 30 kph — might mean the difference between doing it and not. What it will certainly mean is a hugely more challenging mental job ahead.

11 May

Not a bad night really, all things considered (such as trying to sleep at 7000 metres!). There's not going to be any pissing around this morning like yesterday; if the cameras want to see me then they had better get their lenses up the hill.

After 200 metres across the Col the feet are now entering virgin territory for them and for me. I've been higher up before, but the sweep of the slope above and its reputation as an absolute gutbuster has me attacking it with a vengeance. Honest, it's not that I want to be first for first's sake, it's just that it is hard on the head always to be last. I mind far less setting off first and having people pass me all day; at least you get to chat to a variety of people! I learnt that in some of the big road cycle rides I have done; if I start at the back I end at the back, but if I start at the front I end up halfway down the field while meeting heaps of people. It isn't the only lesson I have learnt from cycling; the biggest is how to keep going when it gets tough. So much of this mountain I owe to guys like Tony Catterick, my coach at home, who taught me how tough it is to strive for excellence on the bike.

I sure am needing a dose of that toughness today. Woody catches up about halfway up and keeps pace for a while. I'm pacing myself off a guy and a woman in front who are carrying zip — no packs. Gee it must feel like you are floating without a pack. Mine is pretty light, thanks to Dorji; he is carrying the leg toolkit, the spare flex-feet legs and one other wee bag of bits and bobs. It would be just that much tougher without him. I keep on thinking that some people will think it's cheating, but I figure as long as I never need the emergency stuff he is carrying then it will never be cheating!

The last 100 metres are almost indescribable. It seems that every day you go to a new height there is this rule that the last 100 metres is criminally painful. The slope is steep but it rolls off to only 20 degrees or so, and for the first time ever Russ's tents are the first I see. There are bits of old fixed rope everywhere. Our rope heads right over to a rock bluff and up out of sight towards camp 3, whereas our tents (camp 2) are across the slope over to the left. It sounds easy, but for some reason I feel a great nervousness here. I have been higher, been in more exposed places, but this place has an eerie feel to it. It's sort of like if I try to just stand and balance like the others I will tip over; the altitude kicking in, I suppose.

I may not have been first to get here but for a change I am not last. There's just Woody up checking out the tents. I choose one, more for the fact that it is close than anything, and start to dig it out from the day's spindrift. Our guys probably only left it a few hours ago and already the dry windblown powder has banked up on the sides and door, and snuck its way under to fill up the vestibules as well. At sea level, which is what 3000 metres up in New Zealand would feel like now, this would just be a minor pain in the arse. Here, though, it's a biggie. While many, if not most, people would perhaps just crawl in and not worry, strangely enough I am a wee bit house-proud when it comes to my tent. So I start digging. As I do I can't help thinking, 'If Anne could see me now she would say why doesn't he do this at home!'

Within a few seconds I am out of breath, shagged and getting cold, so I figure that's enough housework and dive in. I realise now that I should have checked out the other tent sites while I had the chance, because as I dive in I realise I have picked the one with the hugely steep front porch! I crawl out to make sure Dorji knows where to come, and quite frankly

11 May 2006 — update from Anne

Place: Home Base — New Zealand

9.45pm and just had a phone call from Mark to say he was safely at camp 2. He said the going was hard but doable, and he managed without oxygen. His sherpa Dorji is carrying a lot of Mark's load and they are sharing a tent; I also spoke to him tonight and told him to look after Mark. Camp 2 is at 7500 metres; tomorrow they will carry on to camp 3 at 7900 metres, and then finally camp 4 at 8400 metres before attempting the summit of 8850 metres on Sunday.

I'm very relieved to see that everyone else, including Dorji and his sherpa colleagues, is finding that last 100 metres as hard as I did. Phew — it isn't just me! That's enough to lift the spirits.

12 May

Well, we are going nowhere for the next few hours, that's for sure. The wind and snow have buffeted us overnight and the forecast, given over the radio in 'Russ-speak code', is for another day of uncomfortable winds up high. We are so early in the season that there really is no need to push the envelope too hard. Anyway, we are far better staying an extra day here at 7500 metres than being higher like team 1 at camp 3, at 7900 metres. They're damned lucky they are not at camp 4, I guess! The advantage of going with Russ is that when stuff like this happens he can see so far ahead because of his experience and knowledge that he can stop us just that bit lower down the hill. Bob tells the story of how they spent days at camp 3 and 4, in 2001 I think it was; anyway, they basically spent too long too high and couldn't finish it off — a combination of being shagged and bad weather.

It is a bit of a relief to sit around. I hop out of the tent several times during the day to move the snow around, but I very soon get bloody sick of that! The decision has been made to stay an extra night here. Our beautiful weather isn't quite as perfect as it was, but it's still heaps better than last season. Apparently you took your life in your hands just doing camp 1 to camp 2 last year, the weather was so extreme. It's only 1pm so there's lots of daylight left to lie around in — hell, I might have been tempted to bring a book if I had known it was going to be like this.

Bob pops by to call his wife on my phone. We each have a team of people at home who are expecting us to be at certain places on the mountain each day — well actually, in one main place on *the* day — so it's important to let them know when we are delayed. I hear Cowboy asking Russ on the radio to ring home with the same message. I have just talked to Anne and got her to post the delay on our legsoneverest.com website; hopefully plenty of families are following our progress there.

Dorji has taken a real shine to my MP3 player, though he's slightly less than impressed with my choice of music. We have brew after brew today; it's time to take advantage of a settled day to hydrate. It's easy to pee here (yep, into the insulated pee bottle — it's too tricky outside; we definitely don't want to risk frostbite to the nether regions this early in the trip) so it's drink, drink, drink.

Once again I thank God that we have Russ's fantastic mountain sleeping bags up here. They're cosy even when you're wearing bugger all; well, for the Penguin anyway. There's quite a lot of nervous excitement as I drop off to sleep. The extra day here was fine but there is only one way to the top and that is to keep going up. I dream of climbing, of standing on the top, of the family and Anne at home especially — luckily it's all positive dreaming tonight.

13 May

Something isn't right this morning. There is no feeling of balance, either on the legs or in the head, added to which I don't want to stick my nose out of the bag. But as always the urge to be early kicks in. Standing here on the tent platforms at camp 2 is scary; the slope just falls, disappears away to the North Col and the glaciers that flank it below. I'm cold and stiff, things still aren't right, and with every step I feel like I'll topple over and slide to the bottom. It's pretty depressing stuff but there's only one way to kick it, and that's to get going.

Compounding the effect today is the oxygen mask. It will be my constant companion for the next three or four days and it isn't sitting right. It doesn't feel right — more like a strange animal attached to my face than a mask. The mechanism seems to work well enough, though; I can see the bag moving in and out, storing the oxygen as I breathe out and delivering it on inhalation (that's breathing in, just in case you didn't know).

It's a pretty cool morning. As always we are all keen to be in front of the other teams that are moving up and down the hill, so there is pressure to get moving — not just from inside me, but from Woody and Shaun as well. Again, even after two months on this hill some of the guys haven't got the concept that you need to be proactive and look after yourself. Don't ask a sherpa to do stuff, do it your bloody self! Some of them still need to be chased along to get their arses out of bed and up the hill.

Today's route is a relatively short day for Everest, as camp 3 is just 400 metres above us. The route involves a scramble that zig-zags up the rocky spur above us to where it rears up into big blocky formations. It is about 20 metres up the last part of the previous day's ice slope, which still feels as scary and exposed as it did before, and then the scrambling starts — short rock steps and ledges, and occasionally broad snow-covered gravel slopes.

There are the tents of the other expeditions' camp 2 everywhere; we are so lucky having Russ and his team selecting the best sites, mainly as they are on the mountain so early. The odd sherpa and climber are mobilising, getting kitted up at the tent door as we pass; Christ, I must appear rude not being able to speak, but the oxygen and the mask turn whatever squeak I had before into a really insignificant squeak now. Luckily either Woody or Dorji are nearby to fill in the gaps and make conversation.

Today is bloody tough. No, not tough, just bloody annoying, sorry. I feel like saying fuck the whole thing, let's go home, why am I here and how come I've been landed with such piss-poor gear. They are all ravings though, really. There is only one person responsible here and that is me, in case I forget, as much as I want to blame everything on Russ or someone else.

I just had a really bad idea. I checked my watch and found that only an hour has passed so far. Today is supposed to be anywhere from three to five hours so I have hardly started! I struggle on for another 30 minutes then stuff it; I plonk my arse down on a rock ledge, unclip from the fixed line and sag, gasping through the mask. Dorji is looking concerned. The poor bugger must think he has really drawn the short straw with me as a client — not just a client with no legs, and therefore no chance, but a soft one as well. Woody and Whetu arrive and ask what the problem is. The answer is easy — I am having a shit of a day, the day from hell. Or as Whetu puts it, 'Don't say you've got a soft moaning pussy of a client, Woody!' Actually, he has right now!

Halfway, I hear them say. A bit past halfway. If they are lying to make me feel better then I'll be pissed off. Soon after that I see some tents up ahead. Now I know from Cho Oyu experience they won't be ours, as Russ always has the highest tents on the hill (yes, I know camp 2 was the lowest, but it was the best site, OK!). This whole day seems to be spent passing other people's camps — tent ledges piled up with kit and oxygen bottles, some with tents up but no one home. What a strange, alien place it is. Yet now I'm up and going again I'm feeling in control, feeling alive again. I'm mad — at myself, at the kit, at the hill. I tell you what, I wouldn't bloody get in my way — moan, bitch or anything right now, I'm firing!

The ridge levels out and a group of sherpas are putting up some tents. Looking up, though, I see that the fixed rope lifts up off the snow and arches up 50 metres or more before disappearing over a lip to what I am sure is our camp 3, one more slope away.

Today has turned into a bit of a race. Some of the others don't want a gimp like me beating them two days in a row. Well, they can think again! Russ has put in place expected times for people to do each day in. If you aren't within your time then you may be pulled from the summit attempt; needless to say, none of them want that. As I said before, it's not that I'm racing, honest, but I must admit there is a certain amount of inner power derived from blowing off your two-legged mates at 7900 metres (I still can't forget that poor sod crying his eyes out below the North Col after I had passed him!).

Yes, again it is the last few metres that really hurt. Jeez, what a long 50 metres up to the tents. I probably made at least ten stops this time. But as I guessed, as I come over the lip of a steep wall there's camp 3 — yeehah!

As I stand up, stretch and look around my heart sinks. Mogens is here and looking very ill. Like Brett, and many others on this hill, Mogens also tried last year, but the word 'try' has different connotations with Mogens. 'Try' involved riding his bike all the way from Denmark to base camp, and then an attempt on the mountain without oxygen. I mentioned how phenomenally fit he is; add the fact that he is an asthmatic to the equation, and you see how tough he is. This time he rode part-way from Kathmandu to base camp, a huge feat in itself, though the poor bugger got struck down with a bug en route. Of any climber on Everest, Mogens has done the most to ensure he is successful. He is totally focused on doing everything right; I wish we were all as focused. Last year he made a gutsy call when he turned around on summit day because he couldn't keep his hands and feet warm enough, a common problem when not on oxygen, as I found out almost to my cost on Cho Oyu. Oxygen is fuel up here.

So to see him slumped over looking very ill, vomiting and on oxygen is a real shock. I do what little I can to comfort him as Woody and the sherpas arrange for him to be accompanied down as soon as possible — the last thing we want is one of our members suffering mountain sickness. One of the sherpas who has just arrived now has to turn around and help get Mogens as low as possible today; I'm glad they are so much tougher than me! So for summit push that's two members down, both from the theoretically faster team 1 — plodding along must have its benefits, I guess.

Camp 3 is something of a refuge, though the slope up to it is dangerously slippery, as we continually point out to Jen, who is wandering around without her crampons on. The tents are on an almost flat part of the ridge. Most years it would be a series of large shale ledges but today it is mostly snow-covered, although the rim of the ledge rises up to insulate you from the sheerness of the mountain. It's high, though — 7900 metres. The others had to spend two days here on the way up, which must have been that bit tougher than our low-altitude nights at only 7500 metres!

I ring Anne this afternoon to let her know that things are on target for summit day on the 15th, a day later than planned. I know it's the day she will be worrying about. She always says she has enough confidence in me and the team not to worry about all the pre-summit day climbing, but summit day is different. I'm worried enough about it, and I can't even imagine what poor Mum is thinking at home in Geraldine. New Zealand is about seven hours ahead in time so I need to remember not to ring her in the middle of the night.

---

13 May 2006 — update from Anne

Place: Home Base— New Zealand

10.15pm Mark called to say that they have spent another night at camp 3 because of the wind. This means they will move to camp 4 tomorrow and try for the summit on Monday. He sounded good, and said that he was using oxygen while moving.

14 May

Team 1 is heading for the summit. Dorji and I have been listening on the radio since 1am when they headed off; it sounds as if they are going to have a difficult day in traffic. We are going to have to make sure we get to the front of the queue tomorrow by getting away as early as possible.

Dorji sure can eat — he has the constitution of an ox! He offers to share some Ra Ra noodles with me but *no way*. Last time he did it just about burnt out my whole digestive system; my backside cringes at the thought. He has carried up two vacuum-packed chicken legs done in a Japanese sauce — from what I can tell, they are for a meal before summit day. He reckons they will give huge power to the legs and lungs, and I can see he thinks I will need every bit of it!

Today is a big day. It's 600 metres vertical up to camp 4, a long day at over 8000 metres for everyone, I think. So guess what — I'm first cab off the rank! Fancy that. After feeling so crap yesterday I feel fantastic today; well, everything is relative here. I'm not puking, so that's a start!

It's really enjoyable climbing today — some straight-out plodding up steep ice slopes, which is normally boring and painful here, but today even that brings a smile to the face. The legs (mine, not the carbon fibre versions) are feeling great; the oxygen mask is working really well. I can hear the valves clicking open and shut, delivering the power to the muscles — I can actually feel every breath in my quads and hamstrings. Making like a sherpa is working great again today, just as it did down on the North Col slopes. The rush and pant method just seems to work so well for me, while most of the others in the team handle the steady pace technique much better.

In between these sweeping ice slopes (they would be steep gravel and shale in drier years) are a series of ledges. It's nice climbing, some of it quite exposed, but here on the edge of the North Face the slope isn't too frightening — just a bloody long way down.

Russ's voice is in my ear, not on the radio but just in my mind, reminding me to stop and look out every now and then. So much of this hill is so hard that the temptation is to shrink inside yourself, battling away with your body. But if only you look up and out you see where you really are — on the roof of the world. Across my shoulder is one of the reasons I am here, Cho Oyu, standing majestically as the highest thing in sight. But guess what, it is lower than me right now. I have climbed higher than the sixth highest mountain in the world and I'm still not at camp 4.

Whetu gives me the usual rev-up about not waiting for the cameraman, so it's time for a break while he heads on up ahead. The other team members are strung out back down the hill. I'm finding it pretty warm today. It was very cold this morning, especially up high, from the sound of the radio calls. As long as you keep moving things are great; stop and things get a bit cooler. It's still far too hot for me to have the hood up, or even have the down jacket zipped up. Looking up, as always the summit pyramid is standing pretty clear for most of the day, with just a few wisps of cloud off to the south.

Up near camp 4 the traffic starts to increase, mostly today's summiters coming down. Lucky buggers — they have bagged it and are now heading for safety, for home. Russ has done it again — yep, camp 4 is the highest of any expedition's tents, just 30 or 40 metres below the bluffs known as the exit cracks that lead up towards the skyline ridge. Ed is waiting at camp 4, where he has been filming the people leaving and returning as well as having the long lens looking up at the route.

If I wasn't nervous before I sure am now. Sitting outside the tent at camp 4 you can see pretty much the whole route up close, right from climbers just above us coming down the exit cracks (I can see Kurt and Marcel, with Terry behind them, I think) to others just below the first step, some actually on the second step and, worryingly, a large group above the second step, where there is obviously a real bottleneck. I can hear Russ on the radio telling our guys to push their way through. There seem to be so many incompetent people up there today that they are endangering everyone else. The guys are commenting on the intense cold, and at least one of our sherpa team has headed down with potentially serious frostbite to the fingers. Others are complaining about numb feet, and this is with foot-warming pads, so it must be bloody cold up there.

It's 3pm and team 1 is back down to camp 4. Dorji and I and some of the others have the Primus going flat tack to melt water and make tea for them before they need to keep on going down. It must be tempting to stay at camp 4, but it is still a very dangerous place as it is so high.

People die here, especially on the way down when they are weakened from summit day.

It's damned scary seeing Terry worried about his fingers. If an experienced, fit doctor like him can succumb to frostbite then I will really be in the poo. My problem, which I have pretty much kept to myself, is that I froze my fingers quite badly on Cho Oyu. I didn't get feeling back into several of them for months afterwards. The problem goes all the way back to Aoraki/Mount Cook and Middle Peak Hotel in 1982. All the fingertips got nipped enough there to turn black but recover; the result is fingers that are hypersensitive to getting further frostbite. I tried as hard as I could to source a glove system that is going to work but I still don't have total confidence. I had wanted a set of the mitts that Bill supplied to many of the sherpas, but for some reason both Woody and I missed out. They were supposed to come up from base camp, but I think no one could be bothered hunting them out. It was my own fault really, as I should have been more proactive and got them sorted well before. It would be so simple if all you had to do was worry about climbing!

As the guys head on down it is time for real focus. Stuff up here and the chance to summit will disappear for good. As just one part of the expedition it is unlikely that I will get more than one chance for the top. Russ will want to clear the kit off the hill as soon as possible, and even if there was a chance of a second go the body would be too stuffed to do it, I think. Right this moment isn't the time to regret not having a higher level of fitness and strength, but those thoughts creep in regardless. I have to force the mind to think how well the body has handled the last couple of days, especially in comparison to the legged people around me, though I know for sure that I am burning up a far smaller pool of resources than they have. Negative thinking? No, realistic planning, I think.

Just having Whetu here gives me a level of confidence and support that money can't buy. I have put so much faith in his advice over the last five years — including advice that if I was tough enough Everest was mine, advice that is coming true by the hour. We sit here looking up even higher, above the second step to the summit snowfield, and amazingly see a lone climber still ascending, this late in the day? Up here it isn't whether you are climbing at night or during the day that matters; that makes no difference really. It is entirely about the number of hours you spend above camp 4, because of the amount of oxygen you have to survive on. What most people don't realise (and as Mogens has found) is that to climb Everest with no oxygen takes more planning and resources than a standard expedition style; you have to spend the absolute minimum of time there or you will not succeed, or worse, not survive. To that end, we have had drilled into us by Russ that from the second we put on our fresh oxygen bottle at Mushroom Rock, just below the second step, we have eight hours to get to the summit and back. Any longer and you run out of supplementary oxygen and your chance of survival drops dramatically, though before that happens Russ will have turned you around and saved your life most likely — that's why we are here with him.

Anyway, back to the guy going up. Hopefully he left camp 4 very late in the morning to avoid the traffic; if not, then he is going to spend far too many hours up high for the weight of oxygen any of us can carry. Good luck, mate.

All afternoon and into the late evening people are coming by, heading down. Many are in a desperate condition after a terribly long day on the hill. Most seem to have no sherpa or team support — most of the sherpa boys have powered on past earlier. At least we know that our guys will stay and help if required.

What a nervous evening! As Dorji and I bunk down to 'sleep' at 7.30 there are still climbers coming down past the door of the tent, all held up by the crowd above the second step. Our aim is to get up at 9.30pm and be out the door, as they say, by 11pm at the latest. We all thought we had that concept firmly in mind, until Max comes on the radio asking when we are going to leave. Woody tells him 1am because he knows damn well everyone else is listening in and will want to leave at the same time as us or earlier. What follows could have been written for a comedy, apart from the fact that it is pissing us all off, which is very easy to do at 8300 metres! Max replies that he thought it was 11pm and why the change? Backwards and forwards the conversation goes, while the rest of us are all yelling from our tents to his for him to shut the hell up. Eventually, after hurting a lot of people's feelings, we get through to him that everyone else on the mountain has just learnt our plans for tomorrow.

It sounds a bit stupid really, a whole bunch of grown people yelling, but you just can't easily pop out and wander around the tents. The site is a steep, exposed slope, each tent has its own platform cut out of the ice (jeez, that must have been a hard job) and there is about 40 metres or so separating the tents. Add the intense cold and the lack of oxygen, and you'll realise that if you have to go outside then you really have drawn the short straw.

My biggest concern was that I would need to have a dump here. I last went to the loo down at camp 3, dangling over the drop while tied to one of the tent anchors. Most people can squat but I can't, the legs just don't work that way, so I need to 'dangle'. It is one of the most stressful and energy-intensive things you can do at altitude, so when it came to eating at camp 4 I was ultra-conservative, keeping to a liquid diet with only a very small amount of solids. Dorji, once he got over the disappointment of me not wanting to share his precious chicken, was the winner — he had a feast.

We set an alarm on the phone and one on my watch. I offer it to Dorji to look after but no way — he will sleep through the alarm, he reckons. Sleep? Bloody unlikely.

---

15 May 2006 — update from Anne

Place: Home Base — New Zealand

The latest newsletter (No. 7) on www.himex.com says that four of the first team summited yesterday (Sunday) and that team 2 (Mark's team) will head off early today — probably mid-late morning New Zealand time. In my last update I said that they had spent an extra night at camp 3, but they had actually spent two nights at camp 2 before moving to camp 3.

---

15 May

Well actually, this should still be the 14th, as it's only 11pm. It's 'off' time already. This is my most hated part of any climb — the start in the dark. I used to love it years ago, but now it complicates life hugely.

I woke just before the alarm, and true to his word Dorji was well asleep. I am actually a bit stunned that I slept at all, but with the oxygen trickling in at half a litre a minute then sleep works. One and a half hours to make a brew and finish dressing, heaps of time — *not!* Every second is taken up with getting the leg sockets on, then the C-Limbs bolted on in the doorway after that. At least I have learnt my lesson and have the crampons already set up on the C-Limbs. The last time I was in this situation I nearly froze my fingers off before I started by having to put the crampons on the legs in these conditions. That was on Cho Oyu, so at least I have learnt something, I hope.

As I am sitting here, though, something strange is happening with the weather. The breeze that was buffeting the tent was supposed to drop right away but that doesn't seem to be happening. It had better not be a windy day or I will be stuffed. The temperature is dropping as well, and the altimeter watch is doing some strange things. The altitude is rising before our eyes and we are sitting still, a sure sign that the air pressure is dropping. This is not a good sign as it means a depression is settling over the mountain, and that means bad weather is on the way.

The stars are still out though, but it's cold — I have never experienced cold like it. I don't believe my watch when it says -40°C. Surely it can't be that cold, though if it is it will freeze every bit of exposed skin. It's definitely time to cover up. Dorji and I check each other's face masks and balaclavas to ensure we have no exposed skin — this is serious shit. Outside, at five minutes to eleven, Woody, Whetu and the team are almost ready. Max and his sherpa have already started up the slope to the exit crack bluffs and I am on their tail. It is far too cold to stand around. But guess what! Tim and Gerard haven't even got out of the tent yet. Today is not a day to be late; there can be no excuse. I guess it is a lack of mountaineering experience, plus the inability to follow the guides' instructions. Every minute they are late diminishes their chances of summiting, simply because we can see a line of lights coming up from the lower tents — yep, everyone else who cared knew we were going to be away at 11pm, and they are hard on our heels.

I get to the base of the exit cracks, the morning's first real climbing, and worryingly the hands are damned cold already. They're not quite numb, but cold. Add to that the fact that I have to squeeze the fingers into the ascender's handle and there isn't a lot of blood getting to the fingertips. Up close the climbing is well within my capabilities, almost enjoyable apart from the intense cold! The short, steep rock walls are mostly iced up so the crampons work well, thankfully, and they are linked by steep ledges. It's great to be gaining height so quickly.

Although I am climbing well I am having several problems with the bloody oxygen mask again. The fit is fine but the valves aren't making their reassuring noises. Thank God for the fixed rope stretching up into the blackness above — not for climbing reasons, but just to know which route to take. As I look down Dorji is within metres sometimes, at other times 10 or 15 metres back. Behind him is Whetu, I think, then Woody and the others. Who knows where Tim and Gerard are. Max is gradually pulling away, going from about 10 metres in front to probably 50 or more metres, obviously on a mission.

The slope eases off, still effectively weaving past rock outcrops on crisp snow and ice — great cramponing. The C-Limbs are really working well. Going up is definitely their speciality; well, mine anyway. Topping out up on the northeast ridge is seriously spooky. Max has moved on to about 100 metres in front, along the flatter part of the ridge, so it is as black as ink. Straight in front is the Kangshung Face, not that you would know it, as it is just a black hole — a very big, very black hole. The ridge dips down a bit then gradually rises in blocky outcrops interspersed with ice cornices overhanging the face. The temptation is to wander along the smooth ice rather than the broken ground, but that could easily be fatal. You will either drop through the cornice, a drop of over 3000 metres, or else the whole cornice will drop. Either way the outcome is the same — you're dead.

At the ridge line we back off the oxygen flow. Russ has us on 4 litres a minute from camp 4 up the steep exit cracks so we can climb fast, even though the body has yet to warm up, though it is unlikely to warm up at all today, I think. When Dorji turns my regulator down to 2 litres per minute it is instantly like someone has put the brakes on. It would be great to do the climb on 4 litres but there just aren't the resources; it would mean having twice the number of bottles taken up the hill.

After what seems like about 40 to 60 metres of open ridge the fixed rope dips down under an overhang with just a narrow ledge to negotiate, with the North Face at your feet. It is here that one of the summit day signposts resides, the body they call 'Green Boots'. He was an Indian climber who perished in 1996, and like most bodies up here his has stayed relatively intact and frozen hard to the substrate. People often ask why the bodies are not moved — perhaps buried in a crevasse or similar. Well, there are two main reasons. The first is that they become so well adhered to the ground within hours of their death that you would need to dig up the mountain to move them; the second is that it is so bloody hard just to survive yourself that the concept of moving a body around is too difficult.

Everyone who attempts Everest is aware of the bodies they will see on the way up. In fact, they really are the markers of the route as much as the rock steps and traverses. But seeing them close up is still a traumatic experience for many climbers. My first meeting with Green Boots is just that — I saw the boots, and some limbs stretching away into the cave. (And yes, they really are green. All I can think is that they look like an old pair of Koflach alpine boots; far too light to be used on Everest when compared with modern boots.) The rope seems to disappear into the cave, meaning we have to unclip from it and walk sort of crab-like and hunched over for a few metres before we clip back on. During this time you are very aware of the expanse of the North Face below the feet in the dark. As we negotiate those few metres I see someone huddled up in the back of the cave. I point him out to Dorji and move on out to clear the route for the others who are following. I try to croak out to the others to check him out; if he isn't dead then he sure isn't far from it, as he looks frozen solid. It is intensely cold and the guy looks only partly dressed, his face black with frostbite, the poor bastard.

Because of the way the C-Limbs are built, with the rigid forefoot, I can't bend over and walk into the cave, it just won't work. Dorji keeps pulling on my shoulder, telling me, 'Move on, Mark, move on.' Right now keeping my hands warm is proving bloody difficult and it is only just after midnight. It's the coldest time of the climb, I hope, but it is already a major concern. I am sure that I hear radio traffic, I can hear someone replying, but it's time to move on as every second without moving is a second closer to freezing myself. Dorji indicates that we have to keep moving. He is getting pretty agitated as it is so cold. He calls out in Nepalese to the other sherpas, presumably about the climber in the cave, although as I don't know any Nepalese who knows? But I am also without the energy to care about it; there is a long way to go.

Seeing the two bodies is pretty disturbing. They are also a bit like a huge wake-up call that this isn't a place to stop; it's not a place to stuff up, especially with the day's real challenges still to come.

Looming up ahead is the first step of the three steps or bluffs on the ridge. It's a big black wall, with the fixed rope going straight up the middle of it — there's no mucking around, that's for sure. Straight up we go. Dorji is right at my heels, sometimes leaning over and either holding the rope tight while I unclip past an anchor point or, if I dawdle at all, he has my lanyard transferred over before I can blink. I'm keen to stop for a few minutes to work the fingers, but no way does he like that idea.

From the top of the first step an easy, almost flat shale and snow ridge leads toward today's scary bit — the second step. But before that is Mushroom Rock, a critical signpost as it is where we leave our partially used oxygen bottles and put on new ones. We now have eight hours at 2 litres per minute to get to the summit of Everest and back to Mushroom Rock to retrieve the cylinder we have just stashed here. There are no names on any of the cylinders, though I have a bit of coloured string on mine. But this is a place of brutal honesty — leave a partly filled bottle any old where and it will be there when you get back hours later — or it had better bloody be.

Dorji changes my bottle for me, as taking the pack off with all its attachments, like the oxygen system and the radio microphone, combined with the down jacket, is just too hard. The fingers are getting a bit too numb now, and I reckon it is the mask. It has been ages since I heard the valves working, but trying to convince Dorji of this is bloody difficult — he just looks at the flow meter, sees 2 litres a minute, and says, 'Working OK.' No it damn well isn't. The valves are seized up with frozen condensation, which is pretty common on most masks. I get him to help me clear them, so in true sherpa tradition he gives the mask a good whack — while it's still attached to the face! My face! On the second whack the exhalation valve falls right out and tumbles down the North Face, never to be seen again. So now I have a hole in the mask as well as the valves not working.

There's no time to piss around though, it is just too cold. Neither is there time to drink or graze on the tubes of PeakFuel that are snuggled up against my body inside the down suit. The really scary bit, the one that I have been dreading, is right ahead, right now — the traverse into the base of the second step. It is steep both above and below, and the knowledge that a mistake here will mean you will drop about five metres until the fixed rope takes up the slack is tempered by the certain knowledge that the anchors will pull and you will take a ride to the bottom, 3000 metres below. I have never been so proud of myself in my life as I move along here, while also being extremely critical of my slowness. There's a real rush of emotions here — controlling the inherent fear of what is below each step of the C-Limb, being jealous of the grace of Dorji and Whetu following — a real mixture of feelings, added to a slightly hypoxic state thanks to the mask.

Almost defying my own belief, I am at the broad ledge below the second step. I look up — fuck, no one told me about this. Everyone talks about the ladder, and especially the few climbing moves off the top of it, but what is in front of me will be harder than any ladder! Above the ledge the fixed rope disappears up over an overhanging wall beside a big crack. It looks like I can use the ascender to help get over it, but I will need to pull up on it while trying some sort of off-camber bridging moves with the crampons on rock. I have finally found a place where my short legs are about to stuff me.

My first tentative go is exactly that, and a dismal attempt as well. Dorji, Woody and Whetu have arrived, and Bob and Cowboy too; I am the cork in the neck of the bottle at the moment. The guys behind me are getting bitterly cold so the only thing is to try and try again, I guess. Dorji's hand is on my arse to try to help, but to no avail. I am hyperventilating like nothing on earth; there's just not enough oxygen getting through to the lungs, and it's affecting not just my power but my head as well. I'm bloody near in tears but I need to get mad, bloody mad. This is about to stop me from summiting. This bloody rock is about to send me home, and that is untenable. It's just a few moves, then I am sure I will be away, though who knows what is above it. Have you ever tried climbing an overhang with numb fingers and hands? Don't — as it compounds all the problems.

Third go. Yes! I flop panting, trying to suck as much atmosphere into my lungs and scavenge every last bit of oxygen I can, but I have done it. I wouldn't have the faintest idea how I did it — I know the knees helped, but I am past caring about the ethics of climbing. I'll take knees any day — up I am, the cork out of the bottle.

There's a large, sloping, iced-up slab ahead, then what looks like a giant's staircase — three huge blocks that effectively have you out over the North Face as they rise up around a big corner. Pretty straightforward, I think, as I try to go as fast as I can to relieve the traffic jam behind. Up ahead is an easy rising ledge, thankfully snow-covered at the moment, to the base of the famous ladder. You have to be so careful here as there are years and years of old fixed ropes hanging everywhere. Unlike the rest of the mountain they haven't been cleaned off by the wind, as they're sheltered here under the prow of the second step. It really does look like a huge ship's prow. Russ replaced the original ladder, which was put there by the Chinese team in 1975, I think, and had become more a death trap than a means of clearing people off the hill. The new ladder is pretty solid, and a delight to climb, though pangs of guilt wash over me. The first people had to have attempted it by climbing the jamb crack to the left — what a feat at this altitude. If my memory serves me right one of the members of the Chinese team climbed it free by taking off his boots and gloves, losing both legs in the process, and his fingers, I would imagine.

The moves off the top of the ladder are pretty exposed but no real problem, though stepping down onto the ladder on the way home will be a different story, I'm sure. It's amazing that people aren't killed right here, as the tangle of old ropes is like a spider's web — a bloody big spider!

What a relief to be over this step, though the word step doesn't do it justice. Up until now, the day has been about the physical — just the effort of climbing, handling the lack of oxygen, the technical traverse — but now a huge switch in my mind has gone 'click'. This is now all down to the head. Up in front is some broken ground, some small bluffs and rock steps to climb over, and then the third and last step, with the summit snowfield rising up steeply. Each step is tough, and I decide to stop for a few minutes to warm my hands and let some of the others in the team lead for a while, but Dorji is pushing me. 'No stop, Mark, no stop.' So on we go.

The fingers are in strife, I know, but it's no use worrying about them at the moment. They won't get any better, but as the sun starts to rise I know they won't get any worse. I take a brief look at the watch (all Dorji would let me take). It's 5am. Another hour or so should see us on the summit, it's so close now. Just as the slope kicks up steeply I see 'Marco', another very disturbing signpost. He died last year, still attached to the fixed rope. Luckily we have a new rope this year but we still pass within metres of him. His eyes are open and staring into space as he lies on his back, perfectly preserved after a whole year. He too is now part of the mountain. No longer flesh and blood, but transformed into a new type of stone. Like so many before him, right back to Mallory's time, the 1920s, he is forever staring out at the procession of hopefuls trudging past.

The summit snowfield is ice covered with knee- to thigh-deep sugary snow. Short legs strike again, unfortunately. The steps that other people have formed, mostly coming down, as there aren't many in front of us, are huge. It takes me two steps and sometimes three to every one of them; two or three steps in sugary, unstable snow that saps the very essence from you.

How come the dumb arse with no legs is leading up here? Behind me are at least 14 or more real legs that could be doing this. I can't yell loud enough though. I step aside and wait a moment or two for Woody to catch up and power on past, but with no voice it is frustratingly hard to get him to understand about the step size, he just motors on up the slope. The others seem less inclined to take over so on we push. Tough? Hell yes, but I will always have the satisfaction of knowing that I have led it.

The fixed rope and steps start to curve up to the right across the slope, heading I guess to what they call the Dihedral. To get there we have another dreaded traverse, not quite as steep as the one below the second step, but on the roof of the world it is still challenging enough thanks. Again, this is the weakest function of the C-Limb. Many moves involve effectively standing on only one crampon point. If it lets go I'll go for a tumble, but best not to think about that. Finally the fixed rope stops at an anchor and heads up some steep-sloping rock slabs partially covered with snow. Just when I am so close to the top, the hill throws this at me.

The crampons are skittering on the rock, and again the knees come into play. I'll happily crawl up this bastard of a hill. This is no longer fun, just terribly hard work, with the nagging thought if you stuff up you die.

There is a crackle of nervous energy. The sherpas and Whetu aren't that happy, I'm sure, and I sure as hell am not. The energy levels are dangerously low; just not enough oxygen is getting though to the muscles, though the brain still seems to be working. I can tell you, any concept of pride has gone well out the door and I am happy for Dorji to do whatever he likes to help. The crest of the ridge is marked by a knob of rock that we call 'Mark's Rock', as it is where Whetu overnighted back in 1996, I think. I struggle with the concept of someone surviving a night out up here, knowing only a tough bugger like Whetu could ever survive it.

I'm shagged. I stand aside to let the rest of the boys through. I have no pretensions about being first on the summit or any other such crap, I'm happy to follow as long as I am not holding others up. I'm too cold to eat, and the energy levels are so low. I know the tubes of PeakFuel are so close, but it is just too cold, too hard to get them out, especially as there is no way I am going to be taking off the gloves to go searching.

The summit ridge is a classical scalloped and corniced ridge — it looks as if someone has taken a huge ice-cream scoop to it. About 50 metres or more up the ridge on the skyline is Max — he must be standing on the top. Well, I think it is Max, but it's hard to tell as everyone looks the same. There are a few others as well. It's amazing to think there were some in front of us; I thought we had left seriously early.

So tantalisingly close, so much hard work still to do. Every step up, especially these last few, will need to be retraced, each step down taking just as much energy as a step up. After a breather it's time to go on, time to tag on to the last of the team. In my mind I create an invisible but unbreakable bungy cord to the butt of the last one to pass me, and I trudge on. It's breezy up here, and in places the rope is arching out over to the ridge to the south. I huddle over the ice axe. I have my hood well up and the cold is still sneaking through. The wind is like a knife, you can feel its thinness cutting right through, hear the low moan as it comes drifting up the North Face and straight through you. The unique squeak that really dry snow makes is the main sound, apart from the laboured breathing of everyone around. Gee, it's a long 50 metres. An athlete could run it in 10 seconds or so at sea level; it will more likely be 20 minutes for me today.

Only 10 metres to go, just the last few metres. I still need to stop several times, but soon I can go no higher. The next step will be down, so I guess I am at the top.

Just before 7am on May 15, at least ten days earlier than I expected, and possibly 20 years later, I really am on the summit of Everest. I really am going to share a footstep with my childhood hero, Sir Ed. It will be just one step, as he came up the other side, but that step is the summit, the one that counts.

I flop down sort of on my side against the pedestal, the table-sized platform of ice that makes up the summit which the others are standing on. Even with just our team and a couple of others (a Turkish woman and her sherpa, I think) it is a real crowd — I can't imagine those days when there are 50 or so all at once. I hug Woody, Whetu and Cowboy, and share an emotional moment with Bob. This has just been so hard, and there is only one thing I need to do — get down damn soon.

Dorji has a panic as I pull off my finger gloves, but that is the only way I can get them in the big warm mitts. To go down I don't need the ascender, just the safety line, so the mitts will work fine. Most of the way down will be arm rapping anyway.

Do I carry the ice axe, or get Woody or Dorji to carry it? Will it be more of a help or a hindrance? Balance is going to be a biggie heading down, so let's carry it, though it will get bloody annoying at times. A quick peek at the fingers and I know I have see the last of several; the last time I saw anything like that was 24 years ago, that white and waxy big toe, and we all know what happened to it.

The radio traffic is crackling. There are loud congratulations from Russ, and a warning not to spend longer than 20 minutes, preferably less, on the summit. I can hear the nervousness in his voice, feel it in my own bones. It's not so much fear as an understanding that I am only halfway. But behind the mask there is a smile, a sense of relief that I have almost got this nailed — the knowledge that I will get home no matter what now. I have my phone but no way am I ringing Anne. As Woody always says, ring from camp 4, when you are more sure of surviving it.

I pull Woody aside. As chief guide today he needs to know about the hands, and I have to make him understand that for my peace of mind I need him to have me on a short rope during the descent. This is especially so down the Dihedral, across the traverse to the snow slope, again on the second step, and on the subsequent traverse to that lifesaving oxygen cylinder at Mushroom Rock.

With the big mitts on to try to save what I can of the fingers I am going to have no end of problems controlling the descent, especially when it comes to unclipping and re-attaching to the fixed ropes at each anchor. And there are hundreds of them, hundreds of times on the way down.

My new digital camera is dead — it's just too cold. Poor bloody Whetu has carried two hi-definition video cameras to the summit of Everest and neither will work. The watch reads -38°C at 7am in the sunshine; a bit cool, I guess. Dorji gets my back-up camera out of my pack, a small disposable Kodak 35 mm film camera that I bought in Lhasa for about $12 on the way in. That was lucky, otherwise I would be on yet another mountain top and not have a photo to prove it. So often after an Everest people want proof — well I'll give them proof! I'm getting a bit shitty — come on, guys, let's go; every second here means the stumps are cooling down and the leg muscles, what there are, are stiffening. I have to get moving. I daydream of a paraglider — imagine just stepping off the summit and gliding on the air currents all the way down to ABC. I saw someone do it off Cook and was very jealous, but it's an idea that might have to wait until next time, eh?

Cowboy strides off down the hill — oh, if only I could move with such grace. Over the radio we can hear that a situation has developed below us. Tim and Gerard are on the summit snowfield and Russ needs to turn them around — they are going too slowly and will not make it home. They left just 20 minutes or so after us but they are now hours behind. Tim and his sherpa negotiate another 30 minutes; if they can make good progress in that time perhaps they will have a chance at the summit. All this because they didn't pull finger and leave on time. Yep, you can blame the traffic for sure, but the only reason there is traffic is because they are late. I can't help feeling sad for them — so close, but no dice.

Listening to the radio, and hearing Russ desperately trying to get the guys to turn around, hammers home the feeling that the summit really is only halfway. As you look down towards camp 4 you know that to die up here would be the ultimate waste. There's no sense in climbing this bloody thing if you can't get back down to appreciate the power it will provide; if you can't skite about it! Again, the mountain demands a new level of intensity and commitment from my mind; you have to be tough, focused and lucky to get home.

Shaun, who had hung back with the two slower guys, has been released by Russ to go for the summit. He sounds as if he has been let off a chain. He is motoring up, probably reflecting not just a different level of fitness but a lifetime of moving as a professional mountaineer in the Alps. This is so difficult for me. As I walk and climb down the easy ice slopes of the summit ridge, the heavy feeling of the pain and mental concentration to come dominates every thought. As we descend there is a long line of climbers coming up the fixed ropes. Anyone who has enough energy congratulates me; the rest just nod. It's tough for everyone — no exceptions.

The radio is still crackling with traffic. Gerard won't turn around. Russ is on the radio, and now Brett gets on as well to try to convince Gerard that he must turn around. As they keep trying to reason with him, it becomes clear that he must be suffering from exhaustion, as well as possibly hypothermia or mountain sickness. Russ confirms the seriousness of the situation by ordering the sherpa to turn around and leave him, as his own life is being endangered. Jeez, what a tough call. My ears perk up as I hear Cowboy on the airwaves joining in the call to Gerard. I hear him trying to convince the Frenchman to do the right thing for himself and his family — take responsibility and turn around, get down alive so that he can come back again. You're a good man, Cowboy. I have my hands full just moving at the moment.

After a stagger and a stumble down the Dihedral's sloping slabs I feel some confidence returning. Dorji is being a huge help by scuttling on in front to the next anchor and then keeping the rope out of my way. Sometimes he puts a wee bit of tension on the rope so I can rest my hand on it and use it for balance, something that is in short supply at present. Woody is climbing down behind me with the short lanyard attached, adding to the feeling of security, just what is needed to maximise speed down this damned hill. Occasionally feelings of relief, a huge wave of

'YES, I've done it!' rise up like a bubble from inside, only to be tempered immediately by the sight of camp 4 so far below.

The traverse back out to the summit snowfield is twice as hard as coming up. The downhill slope is the worst possible angle for the legs and stumps, which are starting to numb up and get floppy inside the sockets. This means the really fine control that I normally expect and demand from them just isn't there, hence the need for Woody behind me.

Finally, at the top of the snow slope, I stop to put sunglasses on. It's amazing how many people get their eyes fried up here. We see that Tim and Gerard have turned around but are sitting down. Cowboy and Bob are down there with their sherpas trying to encourage them to get up and get moving. Christ, if I can walk then surely they can? Russ is watching on the telescope from the North Col, and is constantly on the radio giving the guys a savvy combination of encouragement mixed with a real rev-up. Slowly, with the help of Cowboy, they start moving. I hear them being encouraged with taunts that a legless guy is catching them up — that would be nice, but it's looking more and more unlikely.

Even though it is one of the toughest situations I have ever been in, both physically and mentally, I have still managed to pick up some Everest rock to take home. The thought keeps bringing a smile to my face. When we were young the number one trick to play on someone was to hide a rock in their pack — now I'm on the roof of the world and I've put one in willingly!

Although in some ways the descent from the top of the third step is broken into the same bits as on the ascent, it differs hugely in that each step, each sector covered is one more step toward surviving. Now that I am off the summit ridge this thought has largely gone from my mind, though. The challenge now is to get the pain and suffering that is always associated with going downhill done and dusted, over with. Stupidly, every time the route, the track, goes level my heart sinks (and yes, it is almost a track now, as 40 or so climbers have been over the ground in the last few hours). Every step that isn't straight down feels like a step that is wasted — energy that is wasted, time that is wasted in getting home.

Funnily enough, seeing the other two having to be cajoled and helped down provides me with the power to keep going, no matter what. Woody, Dorji and I are now standing at the top of the second step. Luckily the first few moves are so technical for me that they overshadow the feeling of exposure that you experience hanging out over the expanse of the North Face. Well, they do after the first few minutes of trying to work out the moves. This is where it is critical that you don't get tangled up in the old ropes; there are years of them just waiting to catch your crampons and tip you over. Just these few moves to go, then I'm on the ladder and down off the biggie, a huge psychological step towards home. To help me do those first few moves I think of my friend Martin Hawes and his frog story — basically, if you need to swallow a frog the worst thing you can do is look at it and think about it. Just get on with it, as they say at Outward Bound!

The last part of the step is that bloody off-camber overhang that caused the strife on the way up. It's just a simple abseil on the way down, or it would be if there were not two climbers struggling away trying to climb it. Woody and I call out to them, while Dorji scampers down like a bloody monkey! It seems that these guys have been trying to climb up it for two hours or more, so it is time for them to get out of the way. It's bitterly cold here out of the weak sun, which is tantalisingly close, just metres away from the bottom of the step. Finally, after some more yelling ('Get out of the way — legless climber coming' always works) they are off the rope. There's enough slack in it for me to thread through the figure-eight descender and slide down; the few metres are almost free fall.

What a relief! To stand below the second step five minutes away from Mushroom Rock is almost more important to me than standing on the summit a few hours ago. Now it isn't a case of 'if I get down', but 'how well I get down'. Just as I did when going up, I feel that big internal switch click over. Now it is a matter of grin and bear it, manage the legs and the energy, that's all.

Mushroom Rock. I have no idea what time it is and don't want to look; it makes no difference at all now. Once again, like below the Dihedral, the traverse is much more difficult this way. The reason is probably tiredness as much as anything — that and pride. No bloody way am I going to fall if I can help it.

At last a drink, a tube of PeakFuel. Woody and Dorji pull theirs out as well. What a boost — you can feel the fluids and the energy seeping into the muscles. Let's go; there's no point in buggering around here, camp 4 waits. The tents and people are clearly visible below us now — just a short traverse, some easy ground, the tall first step and then the exit cracks home. I abseil the whole of the first step; again there's a free fall almost at the bottom, but it's so much easier than having to climb down.

It feels as if we have been climbing two mountains. I don't just mean the work involved in going down, though that's certainly true, but more the change in the light. Now that we're in daylight everything looks different. During the descent there has been quite a commotion on the radio as Max and his sherpa have tried to help the guy at the top of the exit cracks, at Green Boots, who we saw on the way up. He sounds close to death, and there's nothing Max can do, although he is trying hard. Shortly we will be nearing Green Boots; I'm not looking forward to it at all. Tim and Gerard are just ahead, after being poked and prodded down this far. Not much further to go now; they'll make it under their own steam no problem, thank God. Russ has again cleared his team off the hill, but by the skin of our teeth, I reckon. Two sherpas are working on the guy — maybe he's Russian? Turkish? Who knows. He is still frozen in the sitting position; no hope of a rescue in that condition, unfortunately.

Shaun has caught up after his summit — like me, it's his first. He is looking pretty fresh and Woody is worried about his toes, so we swap over. Woody heads down, Whetu and Cowboy have both raced on down as well, while Shaun and the ever-present Dorji move at my snail's pace. Jeez, it's tough. You would think that the closer the tents become the easier it would get, but it is almost the opposite. They look so close that you want to reach out, to jump down to them, but there is still probably 30 minutes of climbing for me. Five steps then a rest is all I can manage at the moment. I abseil down the last bluff on the exit cracks and then, and only then, the relief of being off the hill floats to the top. I try to do the last 30 metres with as much control as possible. I hate limping and the stumps are pretty tender — there's definitely some damage of some sort down there.

Camp 4! Yeehah! About bloody time. Even as I flop down and suggest that staying here for the night is the go Russ is on the radio immediately. Get down to camp 3 today — lower if you can. OK OK OK. First, though, is hydration. I desperately need fluids, but the sherpas have just about packed up the whole camp. Only two tents are staying, one for the gear the boys can't carry down and the other for the Swiss guide, Mario, who is planning on being the first guy to traverse the mountain, up from the South Col and down our side to the North Col.

I can hardly speak. The throat is truly stuffed after today, but I try to ring Anne at home. I can just squeak out 'At camp 4, bloody did it!' I'm not sure whether it was the emotion of trying to speak or just the throat, but that was all I could get out.

Bob and Cowboy — you are lifesavers. My drink bottle is half full of ice, which isn't much good, so I transfer some from the bottle Bob has left behind. I suck on another tube of PeakFuel, then get ready to repeat the last four hours, another 600 metres down this hill.

There's no technical climbing to come, thankfully, though the stumps are so sore now that to arm rap down like the sherpas, Woody and Whetu isn't going to work. The back-up plan I have practised for such an event is to go face-in and front-point down, exactly as I climbed up in the first place. I have just realised this works because that was how we designed the C-Limbs — to be excellent at going up (which worked) and compliant going down (which didn't work). Hence the stumps are in much better alignment if I face in. Cowboy has also tried to fix the oxygen mask, as being on half the oxygen of everyone else is taking its toll. Unfortunately, for the first time we have found the limits of duct tape! It just won't stick, bugger it. The only thing to do is head down and go.

There's about 200 to 300 metres of facing in continuously at the start. I need to rest every 20 paces or so; sometimes less, rarely more. Whetu has the camera working again so is back into his cameraman role, and Woody is trucking along just behind. I feel incredibly guilty holding them up. I know both of them could easily be in ABC tonight if they weren't hanging around with me. Instead we are going to be at camp 3 in the mid-afternoon. It would be nice to get down to camp 2, but there is one small problem. Camp 2 isn't there any more; Russ had the boys remove it yesterday. The North Col would be nice, too, but highly unlikely, so camp 3 here we come.

I'm back down to five paces and stop. It's time to make like a seagull again — stop and lift one leg off the ground to relieve the pressure on the stump for five to ten seconds, then swap over to the other leg for the same length of time, then get going while the pressure is somewhat relieved. Repeat every five steps as required — and required it is. The last slope down to the camp takes ages. Dorji wants to pull me down, thinking that it is energy I am lacking, and I just about have to whack him one to make him understand that it isn't energy but stump pain that is the problem, so stop bloody pulling!

The mind is trying to work out how I am going to fix this. How am I going to manage this stump for tomorrow? Well, I won't know until I pull the legs off and see what damage, if any, has been done. I am sure that the pressure pain that is so crippling at the moment is just the result of a long day on the legs. More seagull. Even when I'm only 20 metres from the tent — stop, do the left, then the right, then five more steps. I could probably have run, just gritted my teeth and put up with some damage, but there is still a long way to go, so easy does it. I need to get off this hill under my own steam.

Camp 3. Bob and Cowboy have headed on down, both with frostbite worries. If they pull their fingers out they will get to ABC tonight — wouldn't that be nice! Tim has come down to camp 3 after packing a bit of a sad up at camp 4 and insisting that he stay there the night. Russ has told his sherpa to come down, so obviously he has thought the better of it and he's down with us as well.

The sound of the Primus making a brew has never, ever sounded better in my life. The weather is crapping out, with cloud and snow flurries like most afternoons, so we will definitely stay here — not that it was going to be any other way for me.

Dorji looks shocked when I get the gloves off. The tips of five fingers are white and waxy — the middle, ring and pinky on the right; the pinky and ring on the left. It's tough, but I can't do much about them now, other than be a bit careful with them so I restrict cell damage that could lead to infection. If I can't manage a bit of frostbite who the hell can?

Though I really don't want to do it at all, I take the stump sockets off, ease the liners off and start to peel the Derma-Seal socks off. Oops, the tops of the stumps look great — normally they would be shredded — but almost as a quid pro quo the lower quarters of both stumps are black and blue, tight, with enormous swelling blisters covering them. Shit. There is only one person on this mountain who truly knows the seriousness of this, and he is keeping very quiet for the moment — that's me. I will let Woody know soon. If Whetu needs to add a bit of spice to the filming then I am about to provide it.

It is my responsibility to let Woody know ('Ah, mate, we might have a wee problem here'); just a heads-up really. We certainly won't talk to Russ about it over the radio. A cellphone call and making a time to call and assess it in the morning is the best we can do. It sounds like Russ has his hands full with all the climbers coming off the mountain with frostbite. He doesn't need to be worrying about a slightly shredded gimp who he damn well knows is tough enough to handle it himself.

16 May 2006 — update from Anne
Place: Home Base — New Zealand

Hopefully the next update will come direct from Mark. But if you haven't seen it on the news, Mark reached the summit of Mount Everest on Monday 15 May, 2006. I haven't spoken to him properly yet, just a call that said 'At camp 4, I did it!' before the phone cut out. Luckily Wayne's call to Anne Marie a few minutes later was much clearer, and she was able to confirm that they reached the summit and were back at camp 4, all OK, in fact in 'high spirits'.

Before we know it they will probably be back in New Zealand. Sitting here in New Zealand at 12.10am on Tuesday morning, on my 3rd, 4th or maybe 5th wine, it seems hard to believe. Maybe it is time for bed!!

16 May

Made a huge mistake last night — I left the stump socket liners on my legs overnight (no, that was a good thing) but I didn't squeeze the stumps into the sockets, as in the past it has made them too cold. But this time the swelling has stretched the liners so much I am having huge difficulty trying to fit them back in the sockets. Pain — well, that looks like it might become a bit of a companion over the next few days. Not in the hands — that's plain old frostbite — but while the stumps have a wee touch of frostbite most of the damage has been done by pounding into the bottom of the sockets — something that must never happen just has. In my mind all I can see is a meat hammer being banged for eight hours or so on a tough bit of steak — and the result, unfortunately, looks very similar.

My first thought this morning is that I may need some help to head down from here, but Russ rules that out for the immediate future. He is sending a team of four up, but from ABC, so it's no use to us right now. I am determined not to be carried down — the stumps may be shagged but the arse isn't. Why don't I just slide down? I have been bum-sliding down mountains since I was a kid, and this one will be easier as there is a rope to follow. Woody likes the plan, though we have to think hard about whether Russ will be too pissed at us for cutting up a sleeping mat to pad said arse. Woody does a fine job of creating what he calls my Bermuda shorts — a piece of closed-cell foam mat in the outline of a pair of shorts, which I can then tuck down between my harness and my down shorts. This is mainly so that delicate bits don't get frostbite, and also so I won't shred my down pants.

Woody, Whetu and I have a bit of a discussion about whether to leave the legs on or off, crampons on or off. I go for legs and crampons on. It's a bit of a risk if I catch a crampon point and do some more stump damage or a somersault, but no way am I giving up any chance of independent mobility.

Over the edge we go. If it wasn't such a serious situation it would be ten times more fun, but it is still a definite release to be on the move, under my own (actually, gravity's) steam, with some control thrown in by Woody, my brake-man. With Whetu filming and Dorji carrying some kit we are away. It's possible I am moving faster, with fewer stops, than if I was up on the legs.

Talk about getting strange looks from people on the way up! Lots of people are asking 'Summit?' It's nice to be able to say yes, even if I am sliding past them on my bum at the time. It's amazing what action does to improve the outlook. Every metre down is just that much closer to ABC and home. There really isn't even much time to worry about the future of the stumps; my biggest task is to keep the legs up in the air while sliding, and then trying to steer the body down as competently as possible — which is unfortunately not that competently at times. The aim is to try to always be over the fall line — the 'skier's line' that marks a vertical line down a slope. That's the line a snowball or rock will take if you let it go, and that's pretty much what I am — a large, rocky snowball! This involves not just a simple slide, as often the climbing line runs at a diagonal up the slope, which is no bloody use to me. Why can't people just climb straight up, like I do? After what has to be only half the time it took me to get up this rocky slope we round the corner to our old camp 2 platform. Already there are some other expeditions' tents set up on the platforms our sherpas dug out two months ago then cleared a day before. A couple of young climbers are in their tent door when our little caravan pulls up — not the most common sight on this hill, I bet.

The long slope down to camp 1 on the North Col stretches below, though we won't see much of it the way the weather is going. The cloud is thickening around us as the afternoon storm comes in early. To speed up this bit the ever-inventive Woody decides the 'shorts' have outlived their usefulness, and he designs my next mode of transportation — the toboggan! Basically this is just another of Russ's sleeping mats (sorry, mate, I know they are dear to your heart and purse), this time with me sitting on the whole thing with the end curled up around my feet, just like a real toboggan. With some old fixed rope binding the whole thing together, as well as enabling my feet to push against it and get some steerage, we are ready to go. Big Tim has joined us and kindly offers to help with directing the front, though this really isn't necessary as the front is clipped to the fixed line. Actually it's worse than that, as he becomes a bit of a hindrance each time I run him down. So with Tim out of the road, and Woody as brake-man again, we make the run down to the Col.

The sherpas have caught up after dismantling camp 3 and adding to their already huge loads, and there is news that there are four boys at North Col heading up our way. Finally some help — not that I need it to get down, but it will be ten times faster with them around. We go down anchor by anchor — unclip me, reclip me; unclip Woody, reclip Woody — on it goes. How do I feel? One moment laughing and joking, seconds later pissed off with someone in my way, seconds after that guilty as hell for holding everyone up, seconds after that crying with pain, then the cycle starts again, repeating over and over.

At last the boys arrive, when we are about three-quarters of the way down. It's a relief for everyone as the slope was getting tricky, with a big sideways drift putting strain on the fixed rope. We are also nearing where it gets completely flat, though flat on the North Col isn't quite the same as flat on your average city street!

The boys grab hold of the situation and the speed goes into warp drive. We are flying along. The boys are running, dragging my improvised toboggan, until it gives up the ghost and disintegrates — sorry, Russ, another sleeping mat down. Now what? Do we make another toboggan for the 300 or so metres to the homestead tents on the Col, or what? Or what. I stand between two of the sherpas and dance along as best I can over the narrow undulations of the ride leading into camp and finally down through the tent city to our tents. The boys already have my next mode of transportation sussed — a big tent bag — though it looks more like a body bag for a short guy to me. I sit in it, legs slightly bent but tensioned against the end, and they lace it up. Woody and Whetu make damn sure my harness is incorporated into the lacing; it would be most embarrassing if the bag burst and I disappeared down the slopes to the glacier below after all this effort and time.

With the sherpas in charge I can only sit back and enjoy the ride, and what a wild ride! Over the ladders, bumping down each rung while holding onto the safety line; as long as that holds then I am totally safe, but creeping into the mind is the thought of what happened here a few weeks ago — it didn't hold! But with four sherpas on the lines and having fun what can go wrong? They're whooping, yelling, laughing — what a ride! Within minutes it seems that all the obstacles are nailed, and we're heading down the last slope to another team led by Phurba, well stocked with beers (for us) and soft drinks (for them). Sitting trussed up like a Christmas turkey, supping on a beer at about 6600 metres is really quite unreal, but totally to be expected of a guy with Russ's forethought. It's a mini-celebration with the guys that really matter — Woody, Whetu and the sherpas — another adventure just about caned.

Well, not quite. There is a wee way to go yet. The first part is easy, with Phurba and Dorji towing me across the glacier to Crampon Point. It's a great little jaunt with that sort of horsepower on the front, and each trying to out-pull the other; actually no, it's just Dorji trying to keep up with his powerful boss. As we reach Crampon Point I reflect that it was only six days ago that I came through. Coming back through now, I know that if I ever come back here it will be as a climber who already has Everest under his belt. That creates a very different frame of mind and view of this gateway to the summit.

But what are they going to do now? I see no sign of Woody's improvised stretchers, and I'm very aware that it will be a tricky trip down, and tough. It will be one on the front, one on the back — two sherpas sharing my luckily puny frame.

Nope, within seconds I am 2 metres up in the air looking out at the North Col and the summit. Phurba has put me on his back like a set of golf clubs, just using a head-band to take my weight, my back against his. What an amazing feeling — it is like being levitated on an air cushion. If it was anyone else in the world I would be nervous, but with Phurba on the case I just enjoy the ride. Plenty of people slip and slide down this first few metres but not Phurba. He's all class, and his light, almost jogging gait gets us down safely.

After 200 metres Phurba relents and lets one of the two Tibetan sherpas have a go, since they have been lining up from Crampon Point to carry me. It's a significantly shakier ride on these guys, who are smaller than me, but pride powers them. The first takes me almost 200 metres, until things get a wee bit loose and it is time to dump the load and give the other guy a try. From the start this slight sherpa generated a wee bit of nervousness in me, as I had to be caught as he tried to stand up — just about went right over his head! After a very shaky 100 metres Phurba intervenes; luckily, as the last 10 metres were at a run as the sherpa's legs lost control on the rocky moraine downhill.

Back on Phurba's back for the last bit, from the Chinese camp to ABC. Both were a huge relief, though as always there's a feeling of humiliation at coming in on someone's back. Naturally it is straight to the cook tent, which looks more like a *MASH* triage centre, as members of our team and others are treated for frostbite by Terry, Russ and 'nurse' Cowboy. That guy never fails to surprise me.

As always I minimise my so-called injuries. Sure, I have some frostbitten fingers, and I am happy to have them dunked in some sterile warm water, but keep the stumps in the sockets for now. I need to wait until I get to my tent door before I am willing to pop the legs off and show Terry.

I catch a lift on the back of a sherpa the 25 metres or so to my tent, back to my haven. Cowboy is awesome, bringing up big bowls of steaming water for me to wash the stumps, and more importantly the stump socks. As soon as they are washed it is back into the sockets to control the rampant swelling that occurs as soon as they escape.

Sleep? I think that might even be a possibility, especially after a last peek out the back door of the tent, a peek at where I stood yesterday.

---

17 May 2006 — update from Anne

Place: Home Base — New Zealand

Mark is now safely back at ABC. He rang me last night on his way down to say that he was going to continue to ABC. He said he has slight frostbite to his fingers but assures me it is nothing to worry about. His stumps are very painful, with a lot of swelling and bruising, so he was going to use a sled and yak for some of the trip down.

He thinks he will be in Kathmandu on approximately Saturday 20 or Sunday 21 May and would like to stay for a few days to recover slowly. I am trying to arrange to go over to him.

Keep an eye on the updates; I am hoping that later on today he will be back in email contact.

Chapter 10

The long journey home

17 May

Overnight I have had an insight into what is to come. The pain is just starting to develop in the stumps, and I can see it is going to create a few new gold standards in my life, unfortunately. I lie here in almost uncontrollable tears. I know I have seriously shagged the stumps and am so pissed off with myself. I have felt self-pity like this before, and the one thing I know is to let it out then pick up the strong strands of life and get on with it. That doesn't help too much now, though, as I ring Anne and start to get her used to the idea that things may be a wee bit more serious than first thought.

Terry and Russ assess the fingers and optimistically pronounce them likely to be recoverable. While I agree with them out loud, I know inside that there will be digits gone. Luckily, though, it is only the outside ones, and probably only to the first joint — no problems really.

The stumps — now these they are very positive about, as there's hardly any serious frostbite. That I know, but what they don't know but I suspect is that there is significant tissue damage. The only question is whether they will recover over the next ten days or so, or will the consequences of summiting Everest be more significant? At the worst I reckon there may need to be a wee bit of nip and tuck, but I feel sure the skin is intact, so no problem. They're definitely getting seriously tender today, though. I tried ringing 0800YAK — no, just joking, but a yak ride to base camp can't come soon enough. My biggest trouble today is moving around so I can pack my barrel for the trip home — too proud, you see, to ask for help.

No yak ride today, as Gerard needs the only available rideable yak. So it's a day of contemplating the stumps and fingers — not the best way to spend a day, I can assure you. I have just rung Anne again and broken the news that I might be a bit short in the finger department in the years to come, but that it's nothing to worry about, honest. What a frustrating day! I try a bit of walking, which is a seriously bad idea. I can't even make it to the loo without help, that's the worst bit.

Russ fills us in on some of the dramas that have been unfolding while we were on the way down. The climber who was near death at Green Boots and subsequently died is a Briton called David Sharp. Russ had to hunt through his tent to find out the details; it sounds like no one else was prepared to, even people on his own expedition, though the rumour is that another member of his team has also died. Russ has had to speak to his family in the UK, a tough job but something he has had to do many times before unfortunately. What a tragic year. It seems that most climbers coming off the mountain have some level of frostbite; it's the same from the south side.

Food — now wouldn't that be a nice idea! All I can stomach, though, is some fried chicken Tashi has done especially for me. Terry has me on some particularly noxious antibiotics to prevent infection and they are playing havoc with the stomach. In addition he has me on a maxed-out level of ibuprofen to try to control some of the pain and swelling, though it's providing more help in the mind than the stumps, I feel. I'm bloody glad there aren't any mirrors here; what I can see is bad enough.

Almost packed. Just enough left out for the evening — tomorrow will hopefully be yak day. Thank Christ for my wee hip-flask of whisky; now that is pain medication, or at least the best I can do here.

18 May

Yep, as expected not the most pleasant of nights, but Russ confirms early on that today is yak day — yak express to base camp.

I have been led to believe that riding a yak for six or eight hours will be one of the more painful experiences in my life. Whetu just shakes his head; 'You poor bastard', I can see him thinking. He should know, as he was in exactly the same situation in 1996, ten years ago.

Almost too soon Phurba turns up to give me a lift down to the yak.

Obviously it has to be one that will tolerate a person on its back, and this one belongs to Norbu, a Tibetan yak herder whose son Sunbo is one of our cooks.

Now riding a yak isn't about sitting on the saddle they wear to carry our kit — fortunately, as that's just made out of interlocking pieces of wood — carved wood, but still wood. Nope, you sit behind it on its backbone, padded in this case by another of Russ's sleeping mats — sorry, mate, another one down in all likelihood — with the added comfort of some stirrups made out of climbing rope.

Norbu has the yak on a long lead, and as I settle on its back I know that if I can stay on it will be a good day — it's as comfy as any bike seat! What were the others moaning about? Try eight hours on the bike and six on a yak won't seem so bad.

My first thought is what the hell am I going to call it? Someone is bound to ask me its name. The only thing that's unique about it at this stage is that it is number 6 in the line; other than that I just think of the cattle that belong to Earl, my neighbour at home in Hanmer Springs. We named one 'Wing Rib' and the other, which used to hang round our fence, 'Rump', so perhaps this should be 'Yak Fillet' — at least that is where I am sitting.

Imagine, if you will, a horse with wobbly legs and rollerskates on its hooves — that's what a yak ride feels like. It's disconcerting at the start, but once I remember the few horse-riding lessons I have had so far then no problem — just go with the flow! Norbu lets go of the lead about a third of the way down. I have some control, but the yak knows where it is going. My job is just to hang on really.

Chuldim meets us at the top of the moraine ridge above interim camp. His job is pretty much finished here now. Flasks of hot, sweet Sherpa tea are a great reviver for everyone. The stop also gives Whetu a chance to catch up and get his camera back. I had it onboard the yak for a while, then budding camera-dude Phurba has been roaming around with it, running around even. I bet Whetu is glad to have it back in his hands. I would hate to think what it costs, hence I kept a very firm grip on it while doing the yak thing.

The sure-footedness of these animals is incredible — their ability to recover from a slide that would put most people on their bums, the almost-vertical walls they can climb, even Yak Fillet, with me on his back! The novelty is wearing off a wee bit as we drop down the steep moraine wall to the main Rongbuk Glacier, but just three more kilometres and I will be at base camp, a big step on the trip home. Lincoln Hall and his young client Christopher Harris come by to chat and say good luck (at 15, Chris is attempting to become the youngest person to climb Everest). I slow the yak, though I still haven't found a stop button for it. They have had a week at base camp and are now heading for their summit push — I hope they have some warm gloves and boots!

With base camp in sight, the last 500 metres of the ride is across the flat plain in front of the terminal moraine. Russ's well-ordered camp looks very neat and tidy from this far away. The expected cameras are out — Doug and Si with the Beta-cam 100 metres out — but otherwise I do my best to sneak into camp. Lachhu is there to order everyone around after the obligatory hug. Where do we park the yak? Easy, right in front of the toilet tent as I desperately need to go! That done, where is the bus? The only thing I want to do is get the hell out of here, but I guess it would be rude not to make some sort of appearance at the famous base camp party. Having a film crew along does have some advantages — they organise great parties — but this one's a day away yet.

It is going to be tough to get anywhere near my tent so Russ has me ensconced in the medical room of his homestead tent. That makes life easier, though to do anything (including going for a pee at midnight) I need to crawl — Christ, that was cold, hands and knees out in the snow!

I now know that Anne is on her way. At first I didn't think this was a good idea, but it now seems the best thing known to man, for several reasons. One is that the sooner she knows about the stumps and fingers the better — it will be a relief when she knows, and it's easier to cope sooner rather than later; secondly she needs to see Kathmandu, and what better way than with Whetu's partner Ansja, who knows it well and will be travelling with her; and thirdly, I just might need a bit of support on the journey home!

As I settle down for the night the floor of Russ's tent is bliss. Terry provides some pain relief, and exhaustion takes over.

19 May

Base camp party day. Russ has everyone in major pack-up mode — if they don't finish, no party, which is a big incentive for most. The boys bring my ABC and BC barrels around so I can empty them and repack my kit bags. It sure will be a lighter set of bags on the way home, as I have given much of my kit to Dorji. I owe him a great deal of thanks for staying with a double amputee on the hill. I am sure his heart sank when he knew I was his client; if your client doesn't make the top then neither do you, and the number of Everest summits is an important part of a sherpa's CV. My packs, my altimeter watch and my MP3 player all find a new home with him.

It's also barter day with the yak boys. They all have something to sell, including Norbu. The most valuable thing to me, though, is my yak's bell — that's what I really want. A few yuan, a down jacket and the deal is done. I must admit, sitting on the ground with no legs on is a powerful bargaining position, though in this case I had to force him to take more. Every time I offered more he added more jewellery to the deal; whoa, it was time to stop when the preserved donkey eye on a chain came out. I may need to wait until after I have given it to Amanda or Lucy before I come clean on what it is — about a week of wearing it around should strengthen them for the news, I reckon.

Phurba and Dorji help me into a chair for the party, though I am in no party mood. My thoughts aren't for home or even Kathmandu, but the next night and the day after, the trip to and over the border to Nepal. From what I remember from the Cho Oyu trip it will be tough; there is going to be a lot of piggybacking, which I hate with a passion.

Party time. Amazingly Gerard, who has what I would class as severe frostbite to the hands and feet, is walking around, dancing even — what damage the stupid bugger is doing to his feet I just don't know. I am bad enough, insisting that the legs stay on, but it's a must until I get to New Zealand, I reckon. You just don't want to be stuck here with super-swollen stumps. I make a strategic retreat to my cocoon in the medical tent early while Dorji and Phurba can still carry me; somehow I think there will be few capable of carrying me in an hour or so — you are a seriously cheap drunk when straight off Everest.

20 May

You know those days when you wake up and don't want to go anywhere at all, just stay snuggled up in the bed? Those mornings when everything is so, so hard? Yep, it's one of those. No use succumbing to it today, though, as the bus for home is leaving at 8.30. As I anticipated, there are a few very green people around.

Just dealing with the stumps takes so much energy. Cowboy, Russ and Dorji all help heaps, bringing big bowls of hot water to help me sterilise my silicone socks and gently rinse the stumps. A purple, pink and red rainbow is being added to the black and blue, the blisters are bursting, and the socks are filling with what I call 'stump juice' — gross-smelling fluid from the tissue. Terry still reckons they will be OK, but I have had too much experience of doctors telling me those porkies. I'm happy to believe him for now, though, just for my psychological health.

It's a very emotional farewell to the sherpas who are staying behind. There is a group of trekkers that need to get to the North Col, and Mogens is staying for another go at the summit! He's a real tiger for punishment. I hope he does it well and safe — third time lucky, as they say. The expedition goes on even when we leave. In fact, Russ is just travelling to the border with us, then coming back to manage the rest of the trip. That's his responsibility, even though it means he will miss out on our farewell and celebration dinner in Kathmandu, the real end of the trip for us.

It's a subdued bunch on the bus as we head down past the Rongbuk Monastery, stopping while the monks give Russ and Terry a special blessing for the trip. The monks' respect for them is indicative of their position here — in New Zealand they would be classed as 'good bastards'. The passes that seemed so high on the way in seem just bumps now, and soon we are back on the Friendship Highway. But this time, instead of turning right for Shegar, Shigatse and Lhasa, we turn left for Old Tingri, Nylam, Zhangmu, Kodari and Kathmandu.

Tingri is as much of a shithole as I remember from 2004; we stop there for lunch at the Everest View Hotel where nothing looks to have changed. No way am I getting off this bus — the legs are for show only. I am being ultra-careful in the food department as well. Apart from feeling ill from the drugs, the thought of trying to get to a loo for a crap here is scary — this is the home of the classic Tibetan toilet, a concept that strikes fear into any and all who have used them. Just imagine having to be carried into one of these places then trying to squat to do the business, which is difficult enough on a great day, let alone with these stumps. No way. Brett kindly brings out a small bowl of stir-fry; all the others are having yet another great Chinese meal — the gastronomic journey has recommenced.

This part of the trip is no problem, in fact it's even exciting. You would need to be comatose not to appreciate the landscape we travel through today, from the plain that is the Tibetan Plateau to the narrowing valley at Nylam which marks a 2000 metre descent to our overnight stop at Zhangmu, on the Tibetan side of the border (actually the Chinese side, to be brutally accurate).

Zhangmu has been my worry all day. By the time you have descended down the fantastic gorge through the mist, going from stark alpine meadows through conifer forests and eventually down into the rainforest with its accompanying mists, you know you have done one of the great road trips of all time. The only problem is that you end up in that rotting, musty hole that is Zhangmu, a border town perched on the side of an impossibly steep gorge. It was bad enough staying here last time, but this time it is soul crushing. I know the rooms don't have bathrooms or running water, and my concern — apart from how I am going to get to a loo, short of shitting in a bowl — is the far more important matter of how I will manage my stump cleanliness. Add to that pain levels that are soaring, and the fact that the only rooms are up many flights of stairs — rooms that will reflect the atmosphere here: wet, mould-infested pits.

I am deposited on the couch in reception and just don't want to move. I am incredibly fucked off, to say the least, mad as hell at being stuck here. I would rather stay on the bus if I could. Again, tears of pain and frustration wash over me — I am one seriously pissed-off unit. Why go up to the room when dinner is in an hour? I get a 'lift' on Russ's back to the restaurant next door where we will eat, though being stubborn I take the poles, as after a few pain-relieving beers I am sure I will make it to the loo under my own steam. Stump pain is usually at its worst when I first put a leg on, then after a while the continual pressure deadens the sensation somewhat. So the first weight on the legs always hurts, but then with each step after the initial ten minutes or so the pain diminishes. Unusually, and a wee bit worryingly, this isn't happening; the swelling is just too great, I guess.

Dinner done with I catch an early lift, again on Russ's back, up to our room. I am sharing with Russ and Bob — the old buggers together. They head out to do the Zhangmu thing, whisky, which is the only way to appreciate the place really. Through the open window I can hear the sound ramping up as the night wears on.

It's legs off and a bit of a clean-up using the big enamel bowl — better to use it for washing now, as during the night it is going to become my pee bowl, that I can guarantee. The only way I can control the pain in the stumps is to lie on my back on the bed with the legs vertically up the wall, trying to control the swelling. The pain is past uncomfortable; it's at a level where it is a living thing, like a huge injection of caffeine, stimulating every nerve-end and emotion, eliminating any chance of sleep.

21 May, Zhangmu to Kathmandu and Anne

This morning will be a big challenge, as no vehicles are allowed to cross the border. As always the first job is to queue up. Russ is down there at 6am to be near the head of the queue while the team gets breakfast. Me, I just get the Russ elevator down to the reception couch to wait, only to find it occupied by the receptionist — it's his bed and he isn't about to get up for anything or anybody, especially not at 5.30am. Luckily there is a chair, so the nervous wait continues.

I wish I didn't know what today would bring. I am going to have to be carried down to the Chinese checkpoint, then back on the bus for the 7 km or so down the mountainside through no-man's-land to the Nepalese checkpoint, the Freedom Bridge. I know the bus will not get near it, so I will need another piggyback down over the bridge to the town of Kodari, then down its rough street to our agent's hotel where we will wait for transport.

7am, 15 May 2006, I stand on the roof of the world — you can climb no higher. With the temperature at -38°C, it's not a place to hang around.

Dorji bags his sixth Everest summit.

Just above camp 4 on the descent, still climbing, but even here significant damage was being done to the stumps.

Three of the four Kiwis who stood on the summit that day: Woody, Cowboy and the Penguin; as always, Whetu is behind the camera.

The only way to travel — dial 0800YAK! Not quite a taxi, but a great ride all the same. Between ABC and base camp, the hands were covered to protect the frostbitten fingers.

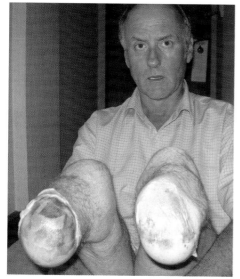

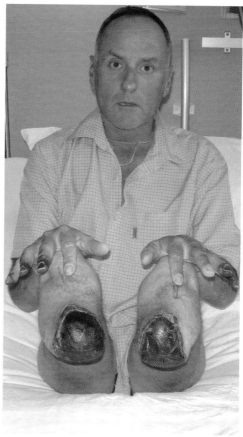

Above Bangkok on the way home, and a new level of pain.

Right Ward 20, Christchurch Hospital, just before theatre to have each stump 'trimmed' by 3 cm. When the black caps were removed, the bones of the stumps were found to be sticking out.

Below Same day: the fingers marked with the green arrows were to have their nails permanently trimmed!

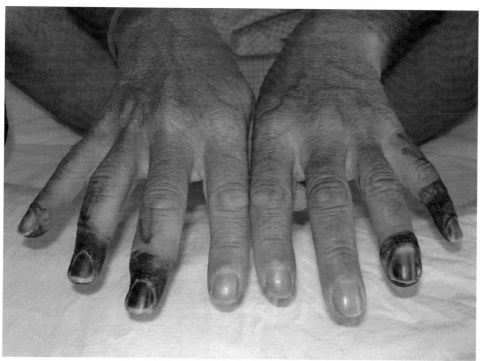

August 2006, the family gather to celebrate our 25 years of marriage.
From left: Lucy, Anne, Amanda, Jeremy and me.

Left In the cellars of Cellier Le Brun. You can still make wine with five fingers missing.

Below Off to swim with the seals, Akaroa 2006, are (from left) Lucy, Ben, Anne, Amanda, Jeremy and Cyndi. No me, as I only sink with the seals!

For a change that is pretty much how it has happened, with the addition of a large dose of pain. Today the stumps are so tender that any weight brings on involuntary panting, almost retching and vomiting — what I wouldn't do for some decent pain relief this morning. The Chinese authorities for once relaxed their zealous regulations to let me board the bus with minimal fuss — thank you from the bottom of my stumps. The bandy-legged porter that has been arranged for me looks barely big enough to carry me without my legs dragging on the ground. I desperately look around the shops of no-man's-land for a wheelbarrow to buy or rent; I assure you there is a lot more self-respect involved in being pushed in a wheelbarrow than being piggybacked. This morning we said goodbye to Russ, as he won't be back in Kathmandu until well after we have headed home. It was a tearful farewell as we have shared a long journey — from Cho Oyu to the summit of Everest, with a long way to go yet, I am sure.

Then it's across the border on the back of the poor bandy-legged porter, and we are in Kodari, Nepal's version of Zhangmu. Here we strike another challenge, as a big slip has closed the road. There will be no rushing down to Kathmandu just yet, but a wait of several hours. A bus has been ordered for the other side of the slip, and luckily there is a four-wheel-drive to get us cripples across to it. The 4WD is a bit too crowded for comfort, with me, Bob, Gerard and a liaison officer, so I bail out back to the bus as soon as possible — room to stretch out.

Kathmandu at last, and I'm getting nervous. Anne will be at the hotel and I desperately want to walk in, but the pain overrides the pride. As a compromise I hobble from the bus down the alley to Hotel Tibet between Cowboy and Bill; it looks like walking, but the toes are just kissing the ground. Anne — what a relief to see her face — she's looking fantastic. After a hug of what is left of me it is time to check out the fingers. It's so much better that she sees them now, and I can sense the relief in her. While the others celebrate in town tonight, for us it is a quiet night in the hotel — that's as far as I can make it anyway.

22 May

While Anne goes exploring in Thamel today, looking for mementos to take home, I decide it is time to get around to the CIWEC clinic at the

Travel Medicine Center to have the frostbite and stumps looked at. Bob and Cowboy went last night, with Bob and Gerard being taken straight there in the four-wheel-drive from Kodari. Gerard has been admitted until is OK for him to be flown back to France, so he must be bad.

My problem is that I am running out of stump socks. I wait at Hotel Tibet as long as I can, but a mid-morning shower has meant that all our washing has got wet, so no socks. I take a taxi for the trip just around the corner to the clinic, a bright new hospital that specialises in travel ailments like tummy bugs, broken limbs, frostbite and mountain sickness — all those unfortunately common factors of life in Nepal and the Himalayas.

My luck isn't so good today. I arrive ten minutes after a chopper-load of frostbitten climbers from the south side of Everest. In fact, they are members of Henry Todd's expedition. They all have frostbite to some degree, though thankfully it looks as though they will all keep their digits and toes. That's lucky, as they are planning on going out dancing and drinking tonight to celebrate their summit, just a few days after ours. Henry has somehow (better not to ask really) managed to hire one of the big military helicopters and flown them all from base camp straight to Kathmandu — now that is service (hint, hint, Russ).

There's a four-hour wait at the clinic — just like the stories of A&E at home really. Add to that the fact that it closes for an hour for lunch (where is mine?) and it feels like a long time. I was due to do some interviews back at the hotel but they will have to wait. I am sure there will be more than ample opportunities for them over the next few days, unless I can escape them of course. The wait also provides a chance for Anne to bring around the socks, but in the end she turns up sockless as they still aren't dry.

Finally I get some attention. The fingers are easy, pretty standard frostbite. I am likely to lose a few fingertips, in their opinion — mine as well. The stumps are another issue completely. They have never struck anything like this, so I become the consultant. With no clean socks though, we need to hot-wash and sterilise the old ones. It has to be done one at a time as I don't want the legs off for more than five minutes or so, or the swelling will mean I'll be legless.

I can see a fair amount of shock in the faces of the medics when

I pop the legs off. Yes, I have been walking on these damn things, and yes, they do hurt like buggery, so let's stop looking and get on with it. They take swabs for infection analysis, and they'll email the results back to New Zealand. This will give my doctors, Dick Price and Sally Langley, a head start on working out the medication. In the meantime they replace all the antibiotics that Terry has given me with fresh supplies, although they are equally likely to make me ill. It's hard to get any sort of food anywhere near me at present, though I do have a continual craving for French fries — finding the perfect fry is a lifelong obsession.

We have dinner tonight in town. I even struggle up the steps to the Red Onion bar for the obligatory G&T before taking the taxi into town. It's a fantastic evening, though I need to escape early as always. Anne and I take a rickshaw back to the Hotel Tibet, the number one experience I had wanted to ensure she had — midnight in Kathmandu, the little guy puffing away, the streets silent for a change — a totally different city.

23 May

An early start for us all as we head for home. Chundlim has arranged our transport to the airport. It's bound to be another day of waiting, but at least it's with friends. Woody and Cowboy are sharing the same flight home, though Whetu and Ansja are staying another few days before heading home. Bill has kindly arranged our accommodation in Bangkok at the Amari, right next to the airport, so I'm looking forward to just lying down on a nice bed, with a nice bathroom — just somewhere that doesn't make any demands on me.

When we arrive in Bangkok the airport staff are great, letting me use their wheelchair all the way to the hotel. And what a room — thank you, Bill! Anne looks out at the swimming pool longingly, wishing she had brought her togs!

The legs come off tonight for what I think will be the last time for a while. The pain of having them on is too intense. The best we can do for drugs is some paracetamol and ibuprofen; I have saved up the last of the codeine Terry gave me for when it really starts to hurt — like about now.

Balanced on the edge of the bath I pull the socks off and almost vomit with the smell of the rotting stumps. This after just ten hours or so in the sockets; it is tough to imagine what they will be like after the 13-hour trip home. To get from the bathroom to the bed I need to stop every two or three metres to lie either completely prone or else on my back with the stumps in the air to minimise the throbbing pain. This time I do chuck up with the pain. The only good thing is that I know pain is temporary.

24, 25 May

Back on another plane. Not quite the last leg, but not far away. The good thing about the plane is that there'll be no media for the next 12 or 13 hours. With what has happened over the last 36 hours I know there will be a reception of reporters when we step off the plane in Auckland and then again in Christchurch.

My most abiding memories of Bangkok are looking at the stumps in the floor-to-ceiling mirror in our room and knowing that things are not looking too hot, and of Anne working away on the computer in our room downloading the hundreds of emails (shortly to turn into thousands of emails) and deleting the nasty ones before I get to see them. Yep, there are some very nasty ones. Just one in a hundred or so, but for some reason I have become the focal point in relation to David Sharp's death on the mountain.

6am; after a long night the phone rings. John, a reporter, needs to see us urgently. Apparently something terrible has happened. Anne scans the news articles for some tragedy but we find nothing. Twenty minutes later John is sitting on the end of the bed announcing that Sir Ed has criticised us for our conduct on the mountain. Something terrible? I think not. We have just spent 30 minutes wondering if Mogens has had an accident as he headed for the summit again, or perhaps some of our sherpas? No, someone who wasn't on the mountain has criticised us. Tough. I'm lying here with my stumps rotting off the ends of my legs, in more pain than I thought imaginable, and I'm afraid the comments from home have little relevance.

As Bob has been quoted as saying, even if it had been his wife on the mountain, my wife, there was nothing different, nothing else we could have done to help. Almost within minutes of having Sir Ed's comments relayed to us come another raft of emails, peppered with more vicious ones this time. It's bloody tough on Anne, who is clearing them. Just lying on the bed during the day and waiting for our evening flight isn't possible any more. I need to do an interview to be sent home for tonight's TV, and radio stations from around the world are clamouring for interviews.

We have breakfast with Cowboy and Woody, providing an oasis of sanity in the midst of it all. I can only thank God that Anne is here with me; it would have been so much tougher dealing with the pain and discomfort, the difficulty of just moving around, without her.

Mike Henstock, a friend from Christchurch, has kindly offered to help manage the flood of media attention, specifically what will inevitably become a real scrum when we get home. Although it's his profession, he very generously offers to do it for nix — just the challenge! In addition, for every probing, negative interview we are receiving hundreds upon hundreds of positive messages. What was probably the most powerful message of support that I could receive arrived with the email flood — a message from David Sharp's family. His brother has made contact, to offer support and to pass on the family's plea to keep the description of David in his last hours to a minimum. They want to grieve for him in peace; the saddest thing is that they are not being allowed to do so.

24 May 2006 — update from Mark

Place: Bangkok

Almost home. The elation of standing on top of the world's highest mountain is tempered somewhat by the media attention that seems to be surrounding some aspects of our climb.

Seems that there are a significant number of experts with strong opinions on survival in the 'death zone', but unfortunately with none of the relevant information. At least 13 people have died on Everest this year. It is an extremely hard environment; a large percentage of the climbers have come away, like me, with frostbite, but have come away with their lives. In every case everything has been done to ensure the survival of all. Tragically, occasionally that hasn't been enough.

My thoughts go out to the families of those who have not made it home. The challenge for the future is to learn from this experience and go out and make a significant difference in the world.

Please join me and my sponsors on this next adventure.

How do you survive 13 hours in a plane with stumps like these? Well, not easily. There are two problems. Firstly, stump hygiene. They really are rotting, so all I can do is use the last set of clean socks and hope they will last all the way home without stinking out the cabin. I'm so worried about this that I take plastic bags to tie over them if they get too bad — roll on Christchurch Hospital. The other problem is that any time the stumps are below heart level the throbbing is almost unbearable; only 'almost' unbearable, because as we know, pain is temporary, a mantra that I chant in my head as an analgesic. To solve this one I fly from Bangkok to Auckland lying on the floor of the cabin with my stumps propped up on my seat. There's just enough room to do it without encroaching on the aisle, and short of some strong pain-relieving drugs it's the only solution.

With home not far away I stop all the drugs, the anti-inflammatories and the antibiotics, as they are both really killing my stomach. I've been on them for nine days and have lost at least another 8 kg, which means at least 15 kg all up so far — a great little diet, but somewhat extreme.

Auckland. I desperately wanted to walk off this plane, hold my head up high, but it is not to be. Chas Toogood is there, and the team from Avanti are there as well, with vans to ferry all our kit over to the domestic terminal for the last hop to Christchurch. Luckily we have a tightly timed connection, so there's no time for a media scrum here, and it's mostly good vibes.

Flying into Christchurch has to be the most emotional part of any trip for me. At last I'm home, or close to it anyway, over the snow-covered mountains, in fact right over our home in Hanmer Springs, and about as close as I am going to get to it in the next few weeks.

The whole family are there to meet us, and we have a few private moments before facing the 60 or more cameras and media people below. Nev is there from Cellier Le Brun with a huge bottle of Summit wine, his brainchild to celebrate my adventure; Simon Hollander (creator of the Christchurch Festival of Cycling, which PeakFuel sponsors) has organised all our bags; and people from all parts of my life, even many complete strangers, have turned up. Russ's sister is here, everyone. It's very hard to hold back the tears at such a hugely positive welcome at the end of ten very tough days. It's two months to the day since I flew out.

I'm home sooner than I thought I would be, but then again, I am not home yet.

One reporter is brave enough to ask how the criticism has affected us, and before I can reply Anne says to him, 'What criticism? Not one person has spoken to us about it, only the media; everyone else, the overwhelming majority, have celebrated Mark's achievement.' What a woman, eh!

The Commodore Hotel in Christchurch, a frequent haunt of mine as I travel via Christchurch, has kindly let us take over a number of rooms for what I had hoped would be some time with the family. But before that there is a media marathon, though thankfully it's orchestrated by Mike. The attentions of the newspapers, television and radio are all a taste of what is to come. I am savaged by one radio host, in the last interview for the day, but I am so shattered I just don't care.

By 7pm I have broken down, with severe shivering, and am almost comatose. Anne is frantically trying to find my doctor but I am determined to have this evening with the family. I finally come out of it. I guess it's just a reaction to the last ten days, the last two months, the last few years, in fact.

In the morning there's a trip to the Accident and Emergency department as instructed. As I feel the doors closing behind me I don't think I will be out of this place for a while.

30 May 2006 — update from Anne

Place: Christchurch

Hi everyone. Sorry I haven't put anything on for a few days; as you can imagine we have had other things on our minds.

Mark is safely in Christchurch Hospital getting expert care. He is going into the hyperbaric chamber for two hours a day to assist with healing. I will let you look up hyperbaric chamber on the internet to find out what it is.

Thank you to those people who have sent, emailed and phoned their best wishes over the past couple of weeks. I intend to print each email and store them with all the other cards etc. that we have received. They have been extremely important in keeping our spirits up over the past week.

Thanks to Room 22 at Paparoa School in Christchurch — you have been with us all the way and your amazing mail has reached us at home, although Mark and I haven't seen it yet; our son Jeremy was very impressed when he opened the mail. It will be something for Mark to look forward to.

There have been a lot more donations made but I will need time to collate them and then I will update the amount on the charity/fundraising page. Thanks to those who have made donations.

Mark or I will continue to keep you informed through this website so keep an eye on it.

I guess there is no way I can escape talking about the media experience that was my climb of Everest, or at least the aftermath of it. It started with a combination of Cowboy's and my own naivety of how the media operates — although we should know better as we have both experienced the positive and negative sides so many times in the past. We both talked about seeing a guy near death; I guess we assumed (incorrectly, as it became painfully obvious) that the media would understand what the last 600m of Everest is like. Even more pointedly, I was so proud of what I had achieved that I made the comment 'previously with everything I have done, someone manages to put a rider on it, tries to diminish the accomplishment — try to put a rider on this, why don't you!' Well, they bloody did.

The guy we now know as David Sharp, the English climber, died like so many did in 2006 on Everest. The day we ascended, he was descending after climbing the previous day. He had been in the death zone for far too long, in -50°C with no oxygen for far too long. His ambition on this, his third trip, was to climb Everest without support or oxygen. His dream killed him.

Apparently I was the only person on the mountain for the two days he was up there, 14 and 15 May; well, that is how it felt as the media storm brewed. Anne, my kids, my Mum, all my friends, let alone myself, were put through a trial: a trial by media, a trial where no facts were expressed, just headline-grabbing opinions. It hurt, no matter how calm and collected I tried to be on the surface as we dealt with the 20 or more interviews each day, trying to explain what life is like in the death zone. It still hurt all of us. There were several journalists — well, perhaps that is too strong a word for them actually — who knew more than I did. Funny, I didn't see any of them at ABC, let alone on the summit ridge of Everest. They were deaf, at least deaf to the truth of Everest. As far as I know they haven't been within a mile of the place. I do know that they sure didn't speak to me. I can perhaps (and a definite perhaps — these people need to get a life) understand some of the misguided talkback callers having the wrong end of the stick, but a so-called journalist hosting the show? I think not. If the media treatment of my climb didn't contravene some ethics in journalism then I would suggest there are none.

Anne and I got a phenomenal amount of positive feedback. The only negatives were a few whacko letters and emails — and the bulk of what was in the media. There wasn't a day that went by without some criticism.

Yes, I walked past someone dying, someone who got every bit of help that could be given that day but still succumbed to the death zone. Everest is an incredibly tough place to survive when even just one small thing goes wrong, such an incredibly hard place to describe unless you have the passion and toughness to go there and experience it. Perhaps we need 'Everest Simulators' to allow people (I can put forward a few names) to experience the conditions, so they can understand?

My thoughts and condolences go out to David Sharp's family. I think it is a crime that they weren't left to grieve their son in private.

Life is about choice. Actually, Everest is about choice: firstly the choice to go, a choice that has extreme and possibly fatal consequences; then the choice to carry on, not to turn back — a choice all on the mountain make. That is the essence of Everest, that is why we choose to be there.

My dream after Everest has been to be able to paint a picture of Everest, the 'why' that is so often asked, the enormity of the task, but at the same time the power that derives from it. That's what this book is about, and I hope what my story is about.

Chapter 11

Reality

5 June 2006 — update from Mark

Place: Hanmer Springs

Well I'm finally home after two and a half months; the last time I saw home was 25 March. It's great to be at home.

Great to also escape the media scrum of the last two weeks; it really has taken a toll on Anne's and my energy. Hopefully as the facts become clear the so-called controversy will disappear. It has been terribly disappointing seeing so many so-called media professionals making statements and accusations with no facts, no research. In fact, it has been refreshing to see the number of school projects that have been sent in that had more research — good on you, kids!

It is back to hospital on Tuesday for theatre on Wednesday to have the tips of three fingers amputated, and more importantly my stumps 'investigated', as they say — opened up, in other words. The fingers are just one of the inevitable results of such a cold day on Everest but the stumps were an unpleasant surprise. They are slightly frostbitten but extensively damaged from the impact of climbing down off Everest. 'Them's the breaks', as they say though; my focus now, apart from spending time with my fantastic family, is to get these fixed and get upright again.

We are still opening the many cards and letters that are arriving in the mail. Many schools have sent in some amazing drawings and letters. It is going to take some time to go through all of these and we apologise if you don't get a personal thank you.

The fundraising for the Cambodia Trust is still continuing and there have been many more donations made which will be added to the charity page meter.

6 June

666 — the devil's day? Actually no. The 6th of the 6th of 2006 is Amanda's 17th birthday. It's a cold morning in Hanmer Springs but mercifully a sleep-in for Anne and me until the first of the day's media calls. Today's target? Apparently I'm clogging up the public hospital system and queue jumping. I don't think I can look at the papers tomorrow; it's all becoming a wee bit much, if not for me then for Anne.

Enough of that, 666 is a day of celebration — Amanda's birthday. I have just had my first weekend at home, and this is my last day out of hospital for a while. We have had a great family lunch, with the whole family together for once, then to cap it all off there was a civic reception in Hanmer Springs! Yep, we had a parade of vehicles from the local outdoor businesses, a lavish afternoon tea, speeches by the local mayors, and most importantly, a meet and greet with the townspeople and all the kids from the school. Gee, the kids have gone to some real trouble — there are posters galore. Unfortunately it is a whistle-stop visit. It is time to get Lucy to the airport to fly home to Wellington, and me back to ward 20 for the big day tomorrow — chop day for the fingers.

I have just been moved into a private room with an ensuite — crikey, I hope no one finds out, otherwise some people are going to moan about that! It's easy to smile and be light-hearted in front of everyone about losing the digits and having the stumps trimmed, but I have underestimated the seriousness of surgery once before, 24 years ago, and I do not intend to let it happen again. This evening it's time for some serious reflection. Not that I can do a damned thing. I just need to remember that when I wake up tomorrow afternoon I will start healing straight away, and not to end up feeling sorry for myself. That just slows us down. It's simply the start of a new journey — the continuation of a life's journey.

Waking from a general anaesthetic is never a pleasant experience but these new drugs they use are amazing. Once you get the pain under control you are up, bright and relatively fresh straight away.

I'm shorter yet again — talk about a slow learner in life's school. I've had 3 cm taken off each stump; the left has been closed up nicely to make a new stump but the right is a problem child. I damaged the end of it so badly that it looked more like the end of a garden stake that had been hit too hard with a hammer. Even worse, especially from the point of view of pain and infection, was that I had stuck the bone straight out of the end of the stump tissue, and exposed bone is the worst possible scenario. The right stump hasn't been able to be closed without cutting the stump even shorter, not a good idea, so I now have a hole, an open wound about 10 cm square on the bottom of the stump. Time is supposed to be a great healer, but I find it is rarely quick enough.

As the days progress my reliance on the drugs that control my life diminishes. While you're on them you think they have little effect, but they do steal your brain. The day I have the PICC line removed will be a major step toward freedom, not just from the daily IV regime but freedom of the mind. The PICC line goes into my veins just inside the bicep on the upper arm, then it travels all the way through to the superior vena cava at the entrance to the heart (yes, I actually have one). That's the big vein that delivers all the blood to your heart, and it can quickly dilute the corrosive drugs that are pumped in. After almost four weeks on these drugs the side effects are starting to compound. Food goes straight through you, and the taste in the mouth is disgusting, like sucking on a piece of rusty steel — not that I have sucked on a piece of rusty steel lately, but I know not to now!

18 June 2006 — update from Anne
Place: Hanmer Springs

Sorry we haven't done any updates for a while. It is like living in limbo at the moment; very hard to make decisions when you don't know what is going to happen.

Mark had more surgery last Thursday — the pinky finger was trimmed back below the second joint, and the middle finger was cleaned out because it was slightly infected. The right stump bone was trimmed by 3 cm. He still has the vacuum machine on the ends of the stump, which seems to be working well, and some new skin is growing. There is still a long way to go.

16 July 2006 — update from Mark

Place: Hanmer Springs

Sitting here tonight in my wheelchair in front of the laptop, I have just calculated that it will take me a minimum of 50 hours to clear the inbox! Yikes! Needless to say, your email reply may be somewhat delayed!

Yep, I'm out of hospital, escaped last Wednesday. So where is the body up to? Five fingers have been shortened, three on the right hand (just to the first joint) and two on the left, the pinky coming out the worst as just a stump that gets in the way. Talking of stumps, how are the legs? The left has had about 3 cm of bone removed and a new stump created, really just another amputation like back in 1982. The right we are leaving after 3 cm of bone has already been removed and some muscle placed over it, which still leaves a wound 5 cm by 7 cm to heal — time will help here, we hope. The stump damage was a real 'surprise'; not frostbite, as many think, but stubbornness on my part in descending from the roof of the world — impact damage.

So that all means another month in the wheelchair at least (OK, three months) but no problem.

Every day brings more ability and new challenges. Anne and I have a lot of travelling to do to ensure we keep our commitments as part of my speaking business. Just because you are out of hospital doesn't mean no medication; every day I need to self-administer IV medicines, combined with a box of pills to ensure things go well. We are so lucky in New Zealand with our health system. The doctors and nursing staff on wards like 20 are fantastic; they often work in situations where there are not enough resources, but they get on with it — a great lesson to us all.

As you may have noticed there have been some negative aspects to my ascent of Everest, but these have been totally overwhelmed by the positive messages we have received. Thanks to everyone that has supported our charity, the Cambodia Trust; check out the 'money rope' to see how well we have done.

Time to do some book writing before I get told off, but before I go a special thanks to Robyn for badgering me along, and also to Peter J. for the most awesome flowers which are still blooming here at home with the message 'Don't let the buggers get you down'; thanks Pete, I certainly am not. Also to my school geography teacher, JB; he brought a framed image of my route on Everest in to me in hospital just when the negative side was distracting me; 'Just in case you forgot what you did!' he said; thanks JB.

Look out for a cheerier update soon, hopefully with a left leg in place. Give me at least one leg and I'll be away on two wheels; no, not the chair, my Specialized Epic bike, which is hanging in the garage!

21 August

Still in the wheelchair, but at least Anne is sending me out around the country on my own now. The wound that four weeks ago was 10 cm by 7 cm has now shrunk to a measly 2.5 cm by 2 cm — almost there! Anne calls this my impatience phase of healing. I have to make a real effort to get out of the wheelchair as often as possible, as I find that the chair both makes life easier (it is a really fast chair, thanks to Ben Lucas) but also harder — it is too easy to sink into wheelchair mode when I need to be in vertical mode!

I have a new limb for the left leg; actually it is just a new socket with the lower flex foot, the ones that I took as spares to the summit of Everest — a very powerful reminder of where I stood on 15 May. Like any new amputee, which effectively I am now, I need to shrink and harden the new stumps before real mobility returns. I am desperate to get back on the hills and on the bike; it's almost criminal to see my Specialized Epic just hanging in the garage!

The journey certainly hasn't finished for me, and will not until I can celebrate the climb with my family, celebrate the adventure by dancing on a table — that isn't going to happen this week or next, but hopefully it will before Christmas. Before then Anne and I travel to the Czech Republic to pick up a lifetime achievement award, which is a great privilege, especially coming from the Czechs, who are the toughest mountaineers around!

The journey has raised over $70,000 so far for the Cambodia Trust, and hopefully the power of what I have done will continue to be used to make a difference in this world of ours.

Keep your eye out for the next adventure — Everests can be found everywhere.

Acknowledgements

As always in life we owe so much to so many and always run the risk of missing someone out — as I will here, sorry about that! Much of the technical information in this book has come from a tapestry that is a combination of my life experiences and my interpretation of information sourced all over the place, especially from the internet. The biggest thanks, though, need to go to two sources: Anne, who has stood beside me for the last 25 years and for a lot longer to come yet, I hope; and the family and team that is the Ahrens Group in South Australia, headed by MD Stefan Ahrens. Without Stef's belief in my dream then it would have always remained a daydream. It wasn't just the dream of Everest that they bought into, but the dream and opportunity to help so many others in the world through our fundraising for the Cambodia Trust.

I have learnt so much over the years from people like Whetu, Russ, Woody, Bill, Terry, Cowboy and too many others to mention, who have inspired me and helped me survive this dream. To Nev and the team at Cellier Le Brun, who created Summit 8850 (buy a bottle, OK!); to Norm and Lorraine who kept PeakFuel storming along; to of course Mum, lucky she doesn't have more than one of me: thanks as always for standing beside us.